X Arette

Pic de Legor

Bigué

Telephon

Spring   Pic

8200

Pic de Coutende

Pic d'Anie

X X X
X
X
X
X
X   8000
X
X
Pic Table des Trois Rois
X
X
X
X
X
X

7575

FRANCE

PIERRE SAINT-MARTIN

The entrance to the Pierre Saint-Martin pot-hole lies close to
the .... miles from the
vill ...., with peaks of
five .... y inhabited by
the .... the mountains
for .... ent belonging
to .... carried up the
rou .... to the French
ca .... ver reaches the
surface at .... d corner of the
map, some three miles from the entrance to the pot-hole.

Men
of
Pierre Saint-Martin

THE LEPINEUX CAVE, where Marcel Loubens fell to his death. Behind the author and Dr Mairey can be seen the inscription to Loubens and the phosphorescent cross placed there in 1952.

Men
of
Pierre Saint-Martin

Jacques Attout

Werner Laurie

First published in 1956
by T. Werner Laurie Limited
1 Doughty Street London WC1
Printed in England by
Surrey Fine Art Press Ltd

Translated from the French
Les Hommes de la Pierre Saint-Martin
First published in 1954 by
La Collection Marabout
Les Editions Gerard & Co

(R 8085)

CONTENTS

CONTENTS

ILLUSTRATIONS

MAPS AND DIAGRAMS

ACKNOWLEDGMENT

The photographs appearing in *Men of Pierre Saint-Martin* are reproduced through the courtesy of the Pierre Saint-Martin Spelaeological Group

TO
MY FATHER AND MOTHER

PREFACE

THE Pierre Saint-Martin Spelaeological Group has
always included a Belgian section because—after
Martel—it was Professor Max Cosyns of Brussels who
originated the work in the pot-holes of the Basque country
and who had studied and explored them for many years.

At the time of the fatal accident to Marcel Loubens in
1952, we had bitterly regretted not having with us a priest to
bring him the consolations of religion during the thirty-
six hours that he lay dying at the bottom of the shaft. Moved
by this a young Belgian priest, Father Jacques Attout, had
in the following year offered us his services as chaplain to the
Group in case another accident occurred in the course of the
explorations.

He was told that he would be welcome, but that except
in the event of grave necessity he could not expect to go
down the hole, as places in the team were limited and
strictly reserved for spelaeologists. His request to join us was
granted, however, and he was included in our team for the
1953 expedition, and from that day he became Chaplain of
the Group.

Thanks to Father Attout, spelaeologists, shepherds,
carabineers, gendarmes and tourists were able to attend
Mass, which was celebrated every morning at the entrance
to the hole, in all weathers, under the burning sun or in the
mist, as well as in the squalls that are so frequent on those
mountain tops.

The rest of the time the " Chaplain of Pierre Saint-
Martin " shared the drudgery of preparing meals, washing
dishes, fetching water and all the other chores.

He also took part in some secondary explorations in nearby pot-holes and thereby won his spurs as a spelaeologist and the trust and friendship of us all.

In 1954 Father Attout returned to Pierre Saint-Martin with the same duties and on the same conditions as before, but he now took a more intimate part in the operations. He learnt to work the winch, became familiar with the intricate technique used in the descent of deep shafts, and spent many long hours at a stretch on the telephone in touch with members of the Group who were going down the hole. In time the day came when, very naturally, he was chosen to play an active role in the sacred mission to which we were all dedicated—bringing up the mortal remains of Marcel Loubens.

Thus it was that on 12 August 1954, after I had spent six days at the bottom of the shaft with my friend Delteil, I had the joy of seeing Father Attout alight at the bottom of the great eleven hundred foot chimney, the first priest ever to come down to the bottom of the Pierre Saint-Martin hole.

At seven o'clock the same evening, he fulfilled his long-held secret wish and celebrated Mass to the memory of Marcel Loubens on the spot where Loubens had fallen and breathed his last, and where his body had lain for two years.

Two days later, our chaplain returned to the surface to receive the coffin as it reached the light of day and to give Absolution on the brink of the hole.

The exploration of these caves is far from ended. It will continue for years to come, and all taking part in it hope to have with them the man whom they know as "The Padre," who has proved himself a valued member of the team by his culinary knowledge, his tireless devotion, his unfailing good humour, his true sportsmanship and by his authority as spiritual leader of a group of enthusiasts, who can no longer do without him.

NORBERT CASTERET

INTRODUCTION

To those with a leaning towards vicarious adventure 1953 will remain the year when three great records were broken; between May and September, man had at last succeeded in scaling Everest, the world's highest peak, he had penetrated into the earth's deepest cave, and had discovered with the aid of the bathysphere something of the unknown mystery of the depths of the sea.

But while from Everest and the Mediterranean successful teams had returned safely and without loss of life, the explorers of Pierre Saint-Martin had worked from the very beginning in an atmosphere of drama. For every time a party left the base in search of new caves it had to pass the temporary resting-place of Marcel Loubens.

That is why the story of the discovery of six giant caves at the bottom of the Pierre Saint-Martin hole differs from others, occupying as it does the period between two interments—the first of which took place at the time and by the wish of those who had been there, and the second by wish of Loubens's parents. There need be no surprise that a large public was deeply interested in it.

When I went to Paris to make my first contact with R. J. Lévi, the organising leader of the 1953 and 1954 expeditions, his first remark to me was:

"You want to come with us, Father? But there are already nearly a hundred applicants and only about ten spelaeologists will be able to actually go down the hole."

Later, when the team had become aware of the difficulties as well as of the dangers, and was getting off to a slow start,

3

letters continued to reach us daily, some enthusiastic, some exasperated, some ignorant.

" I am twenty. I weigh ten stone and offer to bring Loubens up, even though I am no spelaeologist."

Or :

" You are cowards. . . . I will go down in your place. . . ."

Or again :

" I have invented a fool-proof winch, which will enable the ascent to be made without any serious difficulty. . . ."

But as soon as they arrived on the spot, these amateurs with a taste for caving became a little less cock-sure. What they saw was, however, only a very small part indeed of the whole intricate operation; men dealing with supplies, preparing meals, and maintaining contact with those down the shaft. There were men on watch at the winch switchboard, with its red and green flashing lights, and men putting on, or taking off, all the clothes and gear which form an essential part of caving.

As Labeyrie was laboriously peeling off his sixth successive jersey, I heard one paunchy knickerbockered gentleman say quite seriously to his neighbour : " That would be a stunt at the circus, but here it sends a cold shiver down my spine. . . ."

*   *   *   *   *

It is not generally known that the systematic exploration of caves, grottoes and pot-holes has been going on for nearly a hundred years. The discovery of Altamira dates from as early as 1879, of Niaux from 1906, of Lascaux from 1940, and it was about the year 1900 that the spelaeologist E. A. Martel began working officially in the Pyrenees.

The ruthless spotlight of publicity is not always appreciated by spelaeologists, who as a race prefer solitude, silence and obscurity, but by focusing attention on the living science of underground exploration, it has done it the greatest possible service—it has brought it to the public eye.

If every year, when the holidays come round, a few more people of all ages and conditions decide, instead of staying at some fashionable resort, to spend a fortnight twelve hundred feet underground, between a wall of mud and a lake with a temperature of forty degrees Fahrenheit, accepting the prospect of an icy bath, an unlucky fall or a knock-out blow from a stone, all for the chance of treading where nobody has ever laid foot before, of penetrating an enchanted universe of caves so vast that Notre Dame in Paris could easily be fitted into them, and of discovering the first mutterings of civilisation, the good or bad genie of the Pierre Saint-Martin hole can claim a very large share of responsibility.

Chapter One

1950

LIKE THE CUCKOO
IN THE CLOCK

THE underground exploration of this section of the
Pyrenean Massif had yielded some results, but nothing
really sensational. At the spot where, forty years
earlier, Martel's team had gone down to two hundred feet,
Cosyns's party had descended to eight hundred, thus
reaching the bottom of that particular shaft. But they were
still working in the same pot-holes and there was, consequently, no question of any important discovery.

The 1950 holidays were drawing to a close. Labeyrie, Lévi,
Théodor and Loubens had already packed up, and only
Cosyns, Lépineux and the Italian, Occhialini, remained on
the "Gruyère cheese."[1] They, too, had decided to follow their
friends home next day, and they knew that they were
breathing the mountain air for the last time that year; one
more night under canvas and they would be back in the
village of Licq-Atheray in the valley, beyond which their
ways would part and they would go back to their normal
everyday lives.

Seated, their legs swinging in space, at the edge of some
minor pot-hole with vertical walls only a dozen or so feet
deep, Occhialini and Lépineux were watching the sunset in
silence. They were not sure of returning next year to this
wild half-Spanish, half-French region where their tent had

[1] The name given to this region by Casteret on account of the
numerous holes which are peculiar to it.

7

now been pitched for the third successive season, and their spirits were rather low.

Two hundred yards away Cosyns was busy at the camp, but the noise he was making moving packing cases about —the only sound that broke the silence—was not unpleasing;

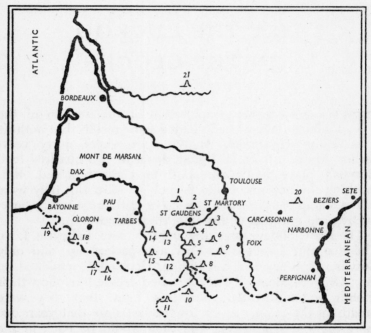

Map showing the principal pot-holes in the Pyrenees:
1. Grotte de Bacuran. 2. Grotte de l'Escalère. 3. Grotte de Montsaunès. 4. Caverne de Montespan. 5. Gouffre de Planque. 6. Grotte de Peyort. 7. Gouffre de la Henne-Morte. 8. Gouffre Martel. 9. Grotte de la Cigalère. 10. Goueil de Jouéou. 11. Trou du Toro. 12. Grotte des Tignahustes. 13. Grotte de Tibiran. 14. Grotte de Labastide. 15. Gouffre d'Esparros. 16. Grottes du Marboré. 17. Grotte glacée Casteret. 18. Gouffre de la Pierre Saint-Martin. 19. Grotte d'Alquerdi. 20. Grotte d'Aldène. 21. Grotte de Barrabao.

as a manifestation of human life it had something comforting about it.

"The fact is," Occhialini said suddenly, fingering a stone he had picked up a moment before, "everything here has been explored. We *know* this Pierre Saint-Martin country by heart!"

He looked over towards boundary post 262 which marked the frontier.

But Lépineux scarcely heard him. At the bottom of the *doline*—the name given in these parts to the short shaft or "funnel," on the edge of which they were sitting—his trained eye had just detected a small opening. Cut in the flank of the rock, it was only about three feet deep, and Lépineux was wondering whether he could manage to throw a stone into it.

"I'm going back to the camp . . . are you coming?" said Occhialini, and made as though to rise.

"Just a moment," said his companion. "Give me your stone."

And pointing to the opening thirty feet below, he asked:
"What do you bet that I won't get it into that hole first shot?"

But the Italian knew his man. Gauging the distance between the thrower and the narrow opening, he merely replied:
"Nothing doing. I'm sure you will."

And sure enough, next moment the stone vanished into the hole.

Then something happened which took them both by surprise. There was a rustling of wings and two crows, disturbed by Lépineux's shot, flew croaking from the hole.

The Italian and the Frenchman stared at each other in astonishment.

"That doesn't make sense!" muttered Occhialini. "Crows always nest above a hole."

"I wonder," replied Lépineux after a moment's reflection. "Suppose there really is a hole, a deep hole, instead of the small one we think?"

MPSM 2*

In answer, Occhialini passed him another stone, and then the two men started to clamber down the *doline*. Ten minutes later they had reached the opening which had suddenly assumed such an air of mystery, but to which no one had previously given a second thought. It only took a few minutes to enlarge the hole, as the rock at this spot was particularly friable. Then Lépineux threw in his stone, in the same way as he would throw a ball, and listened carefully.

For a long time the sound of the falling stone continued to reach him as it ricochetted against the rough sides of the shaft, but he waited in vain to hear it reach the bottom.

As Lépineux stood musing, a hard slap brought him back to reality, and he turned to meet Occhialini's beaming face.

" Up we go! " said the Italian. " We must tell Cosyns."

But when they got back to the camp the professor was not so enthusiastic.

" Estimating depth by sound alone proves nothing," he objected, as he grudgingly followed the other two, with the look of a doubting Thomas on his face.

" You always think you are listening to the stone you have just thrown, when in fact it has loosened others and started a shower of pebbles, and so the echoes from them mean nothing at all."

He was still holding forth when he picked up a pebble and threw it into the hole, bending over the opening and making a mental count of the duration of the drop. Moments later his face cleared and took on the same delighted expression as that of his friends.

" Very curious indeed," he had to admit. " What we need now is a sounding line."

So off went Lépineux to fetch a line from the camp, while Cosyns and Occhialini went on enlarging the opening.

" Here's one seven fifty feet long! " the Frenchman shouted, as he hurried back, throwing a cumbersome package to the bottom of the *doline*.

The lead weight at the end of the steel wire sank blithely into the unknown, and before long the three men began to realise that it had no intention of stopping. The last yard soon ran out and it was obvious that it had not yet reached bottom.

"There's more line in the camp!" cried Cosyns, more than excited now.

But night had fallen and they had to postpone further operations until the next day.

Dawn found the three of them at the bottom of the *doline* with their sounding line lengthened.

It caught up on a ledge once at two hundred and sixty feet, again at seven hundred feet, and then it slid freely away into the depths and went on until it finally stopped at eleven hundred and thirty feet. It was astounding. A smile hovered on their three faces. What had happened surpassed their wildest hopes.

Then Cosyns exclaimed:

"That settles it! We come back next year!" and later that day in the village of Licq-Atheray he sent a telegram to Norbet Casteret, the most famous of all spelaeologists:

Have discovered the deepest vertical hole yet known.

*   *   *   *   *

So began the story of the Pierre Saint-Martin hole—with the chance throw of a stone, strangely like the cast of a dice. Without Lépineux's casual gesture, without the flight of frightened crows from the hole, like the cuckoo from a clock, they would have left the arid spot where they had chanced to stop for a moment and would have remained for ever in ignorance of the existence of the vast unexplored caves above which they had been living for weeks.

And Marcel Loubens would still be alive.

Chapter Two

1954

"HE WAS MY COMRADE"

CHANCE willed it that at that very hour—barely one in the morning—I was by the telephone, the only link between the bottom and the surface. Considering that it was 15 August, the weather was abominable. There was an icy penetrating wind. It had rained, it had even snowed and there was every sign that the storm would start again in good earnest. My post, six thousand feet up, on the bare summit where the *doline* lay, was not to be envied. I had a thousand reasons for cursing and for craving the warmth of a bed, even if it were made of boards. But I did no such thing. Never have I been so happy to be anywhere as I was that night. Not only was I the first to witness the most dramatic moment of the whole operation, but thanks to my presence and to the few simple words that came spontaneously to my lips, a brave man was to rid himself of the worst burden of his suffering. . . .

"Hullo, surface!"

Five hundred feet down Bidegain hung in space, with the container that held Loubens's body stuck fast in the shaft. For more than twenty-four hours the man we called the giant of the team had been working in the pot-hole. But powerful as he was, he was now near the end of his strength.

"Hullo, up there! Talk to me someone, for heaven's sake! I can't hang on otherwise."

So I talked to him.

Yet, till then, the operation had gone well. The safety gear,

12

secure in its place and firmly fastened to the rock, gave us comfort. Everyone was at his post during the long wait before the coffin started on its journey—Rossini and Bidegain at point 260, Lépineux and Mauer at point 700, and Ballandreaux and Brosset at the bottom with the container which Delteil had carefully riveted several days before.

Brought from its temporary resting place at the foot of the shaft, eleven hundred feet down, the body was just starting its slow climb to the surface. It was now 5.27 in the afternoon.

We were uneasy, of course. Wherever we were, by the winch at the surface, on the ledges or at the bottom itself, we all had our eyes fixed on the cable. But the cable was winding up slowly, guided and paid out by Ballandreaux and Brosset, who were doubly careful, because if there were an accident they risked a long stay at the bottom with cold, darkness and anxiety for their constant companions. Our anxiety was due entirely to a too-acute consciousness of the importance of the moment. We had been preparing for it for two years, waiting and passing through the whole gamut of contradictory feelings; hope and despair, enthusiasm and despondency; all was possible, nothing was possible.

What if something should suddenly give way? Nothing did. Everything was all right. Slowly the cylinder rose. At the lowest ledge Lépineux and Mauer, peering down into the pitchy darkness while keeping an eye on the cable and the safety apparatus, could hear the dismal thud made by the coffin bumping against the rocky walls of the shaft. "A real knell," thought Lépineux, "and one which he himself is ringing as though he were the clapper of a giant bell."

From time to time stones fell down the shaft and it sounded just like a storm breaking. The watchers, their bodies pressed against the damp walls, shuddered at the thought of possible injuries. But the cable was pulled taut, whined and then continued imperturbably on its way upwards.

"The small 785 ledge!" murmured Mauer to his companion.

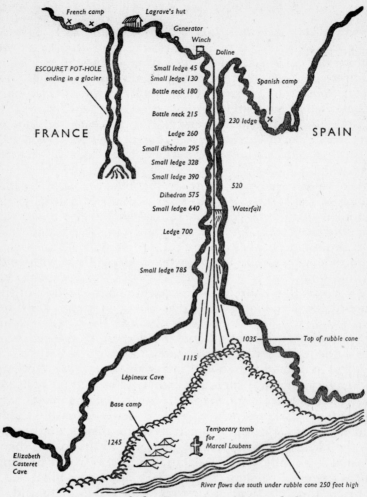

French camp

Lagrave's hut

Generator

Winch

Doline

ESCOURET POT-HOLE
ending in a glacier

Small ledge 45
Small ledge 130
Bottle neck 180

Bottle neck 215

Spanish camp

230 ledge

FRANCE

Ledge 260

Small dihedron 295

Small ledge 328

Small ledge 390

520

SPAIN

Dihedron 575

Small ledge 640

Waterfall

Ledge 700

Small ledge 785

1035

Top of rubble cone

1115

Lépineux Cave

Base camp

Temporary tomb
for
Marcel Loubens

Elizabeth
Casteret
Cave

1245

River flows due south under rubble cone 250 feet high

A cross-section of the Pierre Saint-Martin shaft. It is impossible to convey an adequate impression of the pronounced spiral structure of the shaft and all the innumerable obstacles to be contended with, but this cross-section does give a faithful picture of the main features of the shaft, and particularly of its ledges, which play an important part in the exploration of Pierre Saint-Martin, and in bringing Marcel Loubens's body to the surface.

The container was nearing the first serious obstacle. Quéffelec, an engineer by profession, who was working the winch, had just called the position by telephone. A storm raged overhead, and nightfall as well as bad weather had driven down into the valley below the thousands of tourists who had arrived from all parts, and near the *doline* only the Pierre Saint-Martin men and the Béarn shepherds remained.

The obstacle was cleared without difficulty. Lépineux could still see nothing, as Mauer passed on to him the figures indicating the position of the coffin in the shaft: "740 . . . 730 . . . 720 . . ." sent through every three minutes by Quéffelec. Then, leaning over the edge of the shaft, he suddenly caught sight of the container, and the light on the front of his helmet at last succeeded in piercing the mist and sent back a metallic reflection.

The famous point 700 had been reached! Point 700! It was here that there was a sudden narrowing of the shaft, caused by a sloping muddy ledge, where two men had been waiting for more than eight hours with the profile or pulley-arm.

This pulley-arm was principally the work of Lépineux. Designed by him and made by the pupils of the Technical School at Bagnères-de-Bigorre, it carried a pulley at its upper end, while a steel wire, fastened to a *piton*, or steel wedge, driven into the wall of the rock, secured its foot. Thanks to this makeshift contrivance the coffin should be able to slip through the bottle-neck without jamming against any rough projection in the shaft wall.

It should do . . . but if it did not stand up to the strain required of it, only disaster could follow; and Loubens would go down again to the bottom of the shaft, this time to stay for ever.

Lépineux, knowing this and knowing, too, just how much failure or success depended solely on him, was in a state of almost intolerable anxiety, and literally threw himself on the pulley-arm. How to control it and keep it within the required axis, until the coffin landed on the ledge, was his only thought.

A slow creaking reached his ears. Suddenly, less than a yard away, the cylinder loomed up. But at the level of the rock the *pitons* holding the cables began to bend gently and the pulley-arm to tilt over.

"It's all up . . . damn it . . ." groaned Lépineux, watching his last moment coming with the speed of a hurricane. If the pulley-arm gave way he would plunge three hundred feet to the cave below, to the very one that bore his name.

He braced himself as a new shock shook the whole contrivance. The coffin was now level with him.

"Faster! Pull faster!"

He shouted the order, and Mauer as quickly passed it on. But as he did so a new danger appeared, for as the pulley-arm reared up vertically, Lépineux ran the risk of being crushed against the face of the rock behind him. But up at the top Quéffelec was on the alert and as soon as he heard Mauer's call he speeded up the hoist and only seconds later heard with delight that the cylinder was at rest on the 700 ledge.

It was now half past nine and it had taken four hours and ten minutes to bring the coffin up four hundred feet. On the surface, at the bottom of the *doline*, our faces, though dripping with rain, bore signs of the deepest satisfaction. And yet we all knew, both at the surface and in the shaft, that the hardest part was still to come.

Bidegain jumped for joy, when Mauer told him that the coffin was at rest on the ledge, and Lépineux, sheltering in the recess at the back of the platform, made himself a well-earned cup of boiling hot coffee, with the coffin firmly moored beside him.

Having drunk his coffee, Lépineux unshipped the pulley-arm, and stowed it away; then he unhitched the cable from the coffin and fastened it to himself instead, so that he could be hauled up to rejoin Bidegain who was waiting for him at the last ledge, point 260, leaving Mauer alone with the coffin on point 700.

Lépineux was hoisted up without mishap, though there

was more disturbance in the shaft than usual. "What on earth's going on now?" he grumbled as he set foot on the platform and shook himself like a dog. "I've never seen so many stones falling, nor been so thoroughly drenched! The shaft is nothing but one long waterfall."

Bidegain raised a huge hand towards the invisible mouth of the shaft.

"It's the storm up there," he yelled.

He yelled because at that moment a much bigger stone than the others had smashed against the rock and exploded in a thunder-clap, made all the louder by the echo. He might have added, too, that a stone of that size, landing on a man's head, even though protected by a helmet, meant certain death, as sure as a revolver bullet at point-blank range; but he said nothing, knowing that Lépineux was bound to be thinking the same thing, and Rossini, too, who was on telephone watch.

The pulley-arm was soon in its place, fastened to the shaft wall.

"Up!"

The order to Rossini was passed to Quéffelec. After a moment, the three men saw the cable, which had been lowered once again, begin to move and the slow climb began once more . . . 650 . . . 640 . . . 620 . . . 590 . . . 560 . . . 530.

In overalls stiffened with constant soaking, Bidegain and Lépineux moved about like robots, going from the telephone to the edge of the shaft and inspecting the cable, then listening to the now familiar noise of the cylinder bumping against the rock.

"520 soon," murmured Rossini.

520 was important, less so than 700 and 260, but more than 785. A fissure, known as a *dihedron* and shaped like an inverted funnel and open laterally, turned at this spot into something exactly like a hat, and was very likely to jam anything pointed. The coffin with its encasing cylinder ending in a cone was exactly that shape.

"520!"

Rossini had just transmitted the number given him by

Quéffelec when, without the slightest warning, a terrific roar reverberated through the shaft and the cable quivered and stopped dead.

"The dynamometer is haywire!" yelled Rossini, instantly alive to what was wrong. "The tension has jumped from eight hundred pounds to a ton!"

The container was jammed. For a moment the three men looked wild-eyed at one another. A thoughtless movement could wreck everything. Then, as if suddenly released by a trigger, Lépineux shouted:

"Stop . . . Stop!" and the winch stopped.

"Lower away!" commanded Lépineux. Slowly the cable slackened, lowering the coffin.

"Up . . . Up as slowly as you can!"

The operation began again. Panting, the men, impelled by something stronger than themselves, turned and looked towards the hole. There was nothing to be seen.

At the second shattering roar they shuddered as one man, hunching their shoulders.

"Again!" Lépineux shouted, hoarse but determined. "Lower again . . . Up again!"

But after three vain attempts the coffin still refused to pass point 520.

Up above nerves were on edge. It was after ten o'clock and weariness was beginning to show in fists clenching and unclenching.

Lévi, the leader of the expedition, seized the telephone. "Hullo, down there! What do you intend doing?"

On the platform the three stared at one another in silence. They knew already that there was only one solution, a solution that would entail danger, and great danger, for one of them. They knew that someone would have to go down by the auto-lift[1] as far as point 520 and come up again with the container; it would be a formidable task, back-breaking and almost superhuman, in their state of utter exhaustion.

"Well, we must eat first," replied Lépineux. "Eat and think. This is the time to hurry slowly."

[1] See the technical definitions on page 148.

The three men ate in silence. Never before had they shared so gloomy a meal. They considered the ordeal before them, each finding a thousand reasons for saying " No," and a thousand more for feeling a coward, and finishing up by saying " Yes " all the same.

The technical aspects of the problem became clearer. The " monkey " or auto-lift had seldom been tested. Only Bidegain really knew how to handle it. He had tried it out in the open air last June on a 260-foot slope, and later in the shaft known as the Trou du Chien.

Two hundred and sixty feet! Just the distance between the platform and the *dihedron*. . . .

After the meal, little was said. Bidegain rose, followed by Lépineux.

" Place the *pitons* the width of the monkey."

Bidegain spoke slowly, but his voice was steady.

" Are you going?" asked Lépineux. " If you like, I . . ."

Impassively Bidegain replied:

" No. I know how to handle it. I'm going. We promised, didn't we?"

It was in March of that year that Lépineux and Bidegain had promised Loubens's family to do everything possible to bring his body up from the cave. They had one compelling reason for making this promise: the passage of time had not eased his mother's grief and so long as his body lay where she could not pray for him, she had no wish to live.

Their original plan was to bring Loubens up in the spring and to avoid all publicity. But the weather was so bad that they had to wait until August, by which time the eyes of the world were upon them.

The memory of those last few months was uppermost in their minds as Lépineux and Bidegain waited on the ledge. Then Bidegain, firmly lashed to the cable, disappeared into the depths of the shaft, but not before Lépineux had seen a smile appear on his lips.

And so began the dramatic adventure of the giant from Pau, an adventure that was to last twelve hours. At the end of that time he fell into our arms, a man no longer, but an

automaton with hands paralysed and body racked with fits
of shuddering, having survived an ordeal which, in terms
of facts and figures, was the equivalent of the physical
energy expended by a man carrying thirty tons in a
day.

THE DIALOGUE

As Bidegain made his way down to point 520, one fear
was torturing him. Would the "monkey" wire get crossed
with that of the container and the larger cable crush his
smaller one against a cutting edge of rock, a mishap that
would mean a fatal fall.

But nothing of the sort happened. Shortly before one in
the morning, he reached the aluminium cylinder, with its
head pointed obstinately towards the *dihedron*. First, he had
to join his microphone wire to the copper telephone wire
that ran through the core of the main cable. This was a
twenty minute, nerve-racking job, for the cable was
stretched to the limit by the weight of the container attached
to its lower end.

When he had finished, Bidegain looked round him. The
rock wall was there an arm's length away, wet, greasy and
forbidding. Water was cascading down it and falling ceaselessly on his shoulders. Overhead was night and down below
was night too, total, empty and inhuman.

A feeling of appalling loneliness swept over him. An
irresistible temptation to let everything take its course seized
him. To sleep! To be able to sleep!

Just in time he realised that this first onrush of extreme
depression could be fatal.

And he called up:

"Hullo, up there! Talk to me, somebody!"

I was there.

"It's Jacques, here . . . the padre . . . do you hear me,
José?"

" Yes. Thank you. I felt so lonely. You make me feel better. Now I shall be able to come on up."

Slowly the cable began to move. With his back to the rock wall Bidegain pushed the container with his foot, to prevent it catching in the fissure. Foot by foot the climb went on; it was deadly monotonous.

I lived through it with him. At my side now were Labeyrie and Marie Bidegain, José's wife. They were silent, but I knew that they were waiting, tense and impatient for the sound of the voice from the depths below, the voice that I was hearing and was to hear for another two hours yet.

Until 1.20 all went fairly well. At times Bidegain talked to himself, giving himself encouragement in a firm voice, full of confidence; more often he gave some order: " Up!" " Stop!" He gained twelve feet, fifteen feet, then twelve feet again.

Then he asked:

" Who is up there with you?"

" Here? Some photographers, a few newspapermen, Lévi at the telephone to point 260, Accocce on the generator, Casteret and Labeyrie—they're in touch with the bottom by walkie-talkie, the others too . . ."

Marie Bidegain quickly laid her hand on my arm:

" Don't tell him I'm here. He must stay calm! Do you understand?"

We understood, all of us.

I heard his voice again:

" Of course, it's the fifteenth of August today, Assumption Day! Say a prayer for me, Padre! On Assumption Day God protects all climbers."

All together, we repeated an *Ave.*

He did not finish it.

" It's hard! God, it's hard!"

Bidegain kept groaning. The sound reached me along with that of the container chains, which jangled ceaselessly; it mingled with the noise of falling stones and the roar of the water.

" Father, I can't go on . . . I'm finished!"

My heart began to beat faster. I prayed silently to Our Lord to help me to comfort him.

"Courage, José . . . Come on, courage. You're approaching point 260 . . . Soon Lépineux will help you . . .You'll be able to rest . . . You're doing a great job."

But his voice came through:

"I can't go on."

Lévi came to my rescue:

"José! Lévi here . . . take it easy. Come up hand over hand. Only a little more and you will have done something quite unique. Husband your strength, José . . ."

It was, in fact, by the strength of his wrists—as much as by the help of the "monkey"—that he was raising Loubens's coffin and his own exhausted body. When I took the earphones again, Bidegain's jerky breathing betrayed the extraordinary effort his gigantic frame was exerting in order to bring up the body of a man he had never even known.

From then on things improved. I heard him cry out several times, "So be it! So be it! Thy will be done!" Then, apparently mastering his exhaustion Bidegain made a few yards in silence. All this time I was still talking to him, slowly, softly, making my words no more than a purring, a mere proof of my presence.

Then an astounding thing happened, something that greatly heartened all of us who had followed his slow climb hour after hour. Bidegain began to whistle. And he whistled a popular tune—the tune of a song that in the circumstances took on an unexpected significance. He whistled "I had a comrade . . . I had a friend . . ."

That he had not known Loubens was of no importance, for Marcel Loubens, in the coffin at the end of the cable, had become the tie that bound us all.

Before his memory we were all equal; Casteret, his teacher, the most famous of all spelaeologists, close to my side, murmuring in his delicious Pyrenean accent: "He's a regular monkey, this lad! What agility!" And Mauer, who had been shivering with cold since six o'clock at point 700, with no waterproof and drenched by the water, and the two

MARCEL LOUBENS: a photograph taken in 1951, when the exploration of Pierre Saint-Martin began.

JOSE BIDEGAIN, who played the leading part in bringing Loubens's body to the surface in 1954.

PREPARATIONS FOR THE ASCENT: *Left*: Lépineux taking the profile and other equipment down the shaft. *Top right*: Sealing the container with Loubens's coffin inside. *Bottom right*: The container safely lodged at point 700 during the ascent.

youngsters Accocce and Laisse. It made no difference on this wet and stormy night whether one had belonged to the 1951 team or merely to that of 1954.

Bidegain went on whistling the same tune over and over again. At point 260, which he was now approaching, there was Lépineux who understood his mood; and I, who need no longer encourage him, listened with joy.

If other difficult moments were to come, and Bidegain again grew silent, I should know how to keep up his spirits —not by talking about the present, but by reminding him of what had happened a few days back on our arrival here, the preparations and some of the strange tourists.

A little more and I should soon be singing myself.

I REMEMBER

I can still see myself so clearly, arriving here, *here* meaning the village of Licq-Atheray where the hotel-keeper, Sauveur Bouchet, welcomes spelaeologists and tourists with a smile.

Was it the third of August or the fourth? I no longer remember. Round a table sat Norbert Casteret, single of purpose; Lévi, the leader; Pierre Louis, the mechanic; Vergnes, the cameraman; Quéffelec, in charge of the winch; and myself. And some others, whose features are less clear in my memory.

The village seethed with people, of course; worthy folk who came by car to see the " stars," and asked :

" Is it far, this Pierre Saint-Martin hole?"

" Far?" replied a local, who found the question surprising. " Not at all. At Sainte-Engrâce there's a building called ' World's End House.' That is where the road ends. After that there's a footpath. A three-hour walk, not more."

" Not more!" the tourist would groan. "Not more! That's a good one!"

He would, I imagine, visit the little Romanesque church

in the mountain village, and there his inspection of Pierre Saint-Martin would end.

In the meantime, I tried out my " Tarzan " boots without overdoing it. The heat was terrific. No point in getting over-heated too soon. There would be plenty of time for that on the mountain path, especially as there would be a great deal of equipment to carry. Radio, telephone, what have you. Two mules sank under their burdens.

Lévi had given his orders. We, that is to say Casteret, Vergnes and myself, were to climb by Sainte-Engrâce. The others, under Quéffelec, would go by Arette, and they would take the winch and the generator equipment, dismantled and in sections.

At the same time José Bidegain was busy near Pau, where equipment was being loaded to be dropped by parachute, once our team was assembled on the ridge.

The atmosphere was peaceful. With the little hotel and its excellent cuisine, the tourists' cars, people from the enter-tainment world, the stage, films and politics, there was almost a fashionable holiday atmosphere. Biarritz seemed nearer than the pot-hole. It was, of course, only two hours away by car, while Pierre Saint-Martin meant three hours of physical effort.

The more seriously minded questioned Casteret, the most approachable of the spelaeologists. What they wished to know was what everybody was wondering. Would it be possible this time to bring up Loubens's body?

" I think so; it is the sole purpose of our mission. This year we have all the equipment that we have been lacking before."

" And . . . if you do not succeed?"

The Pyrenean's face grew grave.

" This attempt to bring Loubens up to the surface is the last we shall make. If we do not succeed, we shall not try again. There are too many risks involved."

For my part, with a stock of wafers in my bag, I was determined to say Mass every morning up there. I never doubted that my friends would succeed in bringing Loubens up from the depths of the hole, and I already saw myself celebrating the most exalting Mass of my life; the one which I should say at the top when the body had been brought up.

I did not know then that it would be at the bottom of the hole, at a depth of over eleven hundred feet, that I should celebrate my most impressive Mass. . . .

THE COFFIN DROPS FROM THE SKY

My idea had been that I would talk to José Bidegain about things like that, as he wrestled with the container in a narrow part of the chimney. The cable was beginning to untwist, spinning the cylinder and José with it in a dizzy waltz. As he swung helplessly against the rough rock walls, his back was scraped and bruised, and then he had to clamber the length of the container to free it. . . .

I wondered whether it was the moment to amuse him with a description of the tourists sweating up the mountain track, or of the pleasure one feels on approaching a fountain. No, I thought, that would be quite wrong, when he was half dead with fatigue, and drenched with icy water pouring down on him from every side.

Suddenly I remembered the aeroplanes, and that it was José who had been sent to Pau to supervise the loading of the parachutes. The memory of that day came back to me quite naturally and I began to describe it with enthusiasm.

" Do you remember, José, how anxious you were when the gear did not arrive for marking where the parachutes were to drop?"

I can still see him so clearly. That immense figure standing between the white, green and yellow tents pitched on the bare ridge was thoroughly uneasy. " God in Heaven. Where on earth are they dawdling? The planes will soon be overhead and they won't find a single guide-mark."

Then, sure enough, Bidegain had an idea.

" Bruno," he fired suddenly at an astonished journalist.
" Quick. Give me your overalls! "

" Why? Do you like them? "

" It's not for me. For the planes."

I understood. He was going to take some article of clothing or other from everybody and make a highly individual
signalling system. At the end of twenty minutes or so every
man had been relieved of something, a pullover here, a shirt
there.

The sacrifice was in vain. For the team with the marking
gear arrived at last and they had soon laid out on the dropping zone an immense T of white cloth to show the direction
of the wind.

Soon the Junkers appeared in the blue sky. They circled
round for some time, a beautiful sight to our admiring eyes.
Four tons of gear were dropped on forty-six parachutes of
every conceivable colour. There was just one critical moment
near the end of the drop. The pulleys which were needed
for bringing up the coffin were still to come. The plane flew
too high and, when the pilot launched the two pulley-arms,
the parachute opened late and there was a heavy crash.

" Good God, let's hope they don't do that with the container! "

It was Bidegain's voice again. He had just inspected the
pulley-arms and seen that it was possible to repair them. But
the container was another matter.

Everyone looked a little anxious. The plane purred and
turned above our heads. And there it was! Fastened to two
parachutes the coffin fell from the sky quickly and heavily.
The morning sun had barely time to play on its silver
surface.

Suddenly a great hush fell over the mountain. There was
no sound but that of the engine overhead. Our hearts beat
faster and we all stood rigid as statues, but statues that some
strange master of ceremonies had arranged with their faces
all turned towards the same spot—the dropping ground.

It needed the impact, violent as it was, to bring us to our
senses. Everyone had so far stood there without moving and

left the parachutes where they had fallen; now as though released by a spring they all rushed forward.

Lévi, Bidegain, Casteret and Lépineux were the first to reach the container and it was Lévi who said:

" Splendid, it's intact. Great chaps, these airmen!"

Tourists and newspapermen were already coming up, and there were willing hands offering to help.

Lévi, always the same Lévi, small, highly-strung, commanding, very much the leader, refused all their offers.

" No, no . . . I only wish members of the expedition to carry the container . . . I must have responsible bearers." With the other equipment it was stored away in the hut of a shepherd called Lagrave, near the entrance to the pot-hole.

Everything was ready at last at the top, and the first descent of 1954 could now be made. This honour again fell to Lépineux.

It was an honour, of course, but it was also a risk. This first descent had to be made by an experienced and hardened spelaeologist. During the winter, stones became loose and balanced precariously on the ledges, where dangerous piles of them would often accumulate. The first descent had to be a combined reconnaissance and cleaning up operation.

There was more to it than that. While one group, consisting of Quéffelec the engineer, Pierre Louis the mechanic, Rossini, Laisse and Accocce, was busy assembling the winch, others were unrolling the cable and laying it out between the hut and the *doline*.

" You see," said Bidegain. " It has to be unwound carefully. The first man to go down will get a rapid spinning movement in any case, particularly at point 785, and he will have a bad time if he suffers from dizziness. It's a bad moment that, always."

I glanced at Lépineux, He was laughing. His eyes were never still and with a quaint rimless helmet on his head he looked like the comedian of the party. Yet, with Casteret and Bidegain, he was the most serious of them all, and the most experienced. The first cave at the bottom of the Pierre Saint-Martin shaft is called, quite appropriately, Lépineux cave. He was a mystic of spelaeology, or perhaps just a plain mystic. His real life lay down below in the mud and cold; it was there that it took on a meaning for him.

Lépineux's descent was fixed for dawn next day. Before dropping off to sleep in the tent, tired out, we took a last look at the scene around us. Pessimists looked at the sky, a starless sky, where ugly clouds were gathering. " A storm tonight," they murmured.

The poets and enthusiasts liked to look over towards the valleys, where the lights of Sainte-Engrâce twinkled in the distance. "And there," said someone, stretching out an arm, " is Bagnères-de-Bigorre, the little village where they made the pulley-arms."

The picture of those tiny villages so far away, yet brought seemingly so close by their lights, and sleeping securely in the Pyrenean night, reminded us of the world below and warmed my heart as I closed my eyes.

TWO OPPOSING THESES

Silhouetted against the light stood three Spanish gendarmes. Dawn had not yet broken as Lépineux made his way to the *doline*.

Let's hope it was nothing serious. There was a dispute as to which country owned the entrance to the caves. Suppose the Spaniards bluntly refused to let us go down the hole?

Then along came Lévi.

" Well, gentlemen, what can I do for you?"

After the customary greetings, exchanged with exquisite politeness, which means nothing, one of the Spaniards, who was obviously an officer, said:

" You are the leader, are you not? Would you give me a complete list of the members of your party?"

" Yes, certainly. Do you wish to check up on us?"

The officer smiled:

" Not at all, if by that you mean a third degree. All we

wish to do is to celebrate your first trip down the pot-hole
by inviting you to share our dinner today."

Lévi's face brightened. Our neighbour's intentions were
evidently friendly.

"Of course we accept! My friends and I will be happy
to pass a pleasant hour in your company."

"Well," said the officer, a man of decided charm, "we
shall be delighted to send you up supplies of food every
other day, not forgetting the wine and the anisette!"

And after that they went away.

A little later, while Lépineux was at work in the shaft,
inspecting the walls and clearing away the debris of broken
stones caused by erosion during the winter, Lévi and
Casteret stood at the edge of the *doline*, discussing the most
important part of the operation—the recovery of Marcel
Loubens's body. The technicians soon joined them.

"In my opinion," stated Quéffelec, who had invented the
winch and worked it on the two previous expeditions, "the
best plan is to hoist the body up on the cable, while an
escorting party circles the cylinder, and guides it towards
the top of the shaft. The escort would obviously use the
auto-lifts that Bidegain tried out with me last June."

But Norbert Casteret shook his head.

"Maybe I'm old-fashioned," he said with a smile, "and
like to stick to old methods; all the same, I feel past experience is best and that we should choose the simplest way
possible. In my view this has always been, and still is, to use
ladders. Do you remember the work of the Lyons scouts in
1952? It was wonderful."

"Maybe, but of little practical use in the present case,"
said Quéffelec.

"Agreed. Still I propose to fix men securely to the ledges
with *pitons* at the dangerous points, and to hoist the cylinder
by winch without any human escort, or at least with none
hanging in the shaft, though there would be several small
parties stationed at carefully chosen points."

The argument was still going on when Lépineux came up
from his task of clearing the shaft.

The kit Casteret was wearing was a model. Round his neck he wore a rubber band to stop the icy water running down his back, and there were rubber bands on his wrists, too.

"It's a great improvement," he claimed.

Some of the younger men tried to make fun of his get-up. That would soon pass. When they had had a few hours standing under falling water, they would be sorry they had not followed Casteret's advice.

With Casteret leading, others were to follow him down to the bottom of the shaft, each taking some piece of equipment that would be of use in bringing the cylinder up safely, the telephone for the bottom of the shaft, boards for flooring the ledges, tools, food and ropes.

Before going down, Casteret took me into his confidence:

"There is nothing in going down there. No real difficulties. But when you have to stay down there alone, cut off from the surface, then it gets you. The silence overpowers you. The great mass of rocks weighs on you. You breathe with difficulty, and I can assure you that you are more than delighted when someone joins you. Once you know he is coming down the shaft, you shout and try to make yourself heard. Whatever we may say, man is a social animal."

But I, who had never been down the shaft and was so eager to know how it felt down there, did not understand his feelings. Or rather I did not want to. I still felt envious of the man who was lashed to the end of the cable and being lowered down so gently. Even when he cried: "Stop! Stop!" when the winch cable, freed from all friction, began to unravel and brought on an attack of giddiness as he was making his way into the Lépineux cave where Loubens had lain for two years, sleeping the sleep of eternity, I only thought: "How lucky he is, he's at the bottom now!"

I gave no thought to Loubens, who had died so tragically, nor to Delteil who had just gone down with the coffin and narrowly escaped the same fate. This brave Pyrenean had passed the most dangerous points, overcome all the difficulties, when suddenly, as he neared the bottom, he saw an unusual play in his harness straps. His face broke out in a cold sweat. "If it snaps," he thought, "I shall fall with the coffin and have to share it with Loubens." He did not exaggerate, for the straps that held him to the cable were coming undone. He grit his teeth and in a state bordering almost on trance, adjusted the straps in time. Had he given all his attention to the container it would have been the end of him.

All this I knew, but it was my turn to fetch the water that day and walking down the treeless footpath towards the troughs, I dreamt of that damp, black cave, like the child who must have a coveted toy and cannot be denied.

At Pierre Saint-Martin itself there is no water; the country is completely arid. To get a supply involves a trip down the mountain side almost to the edge of the forest. Troughs built by the shepherds await the traveller in search of water; some of them very simple, like those of La Salière and La Bigué, others decorated in amusing style like that of Coum. The shepherds have made him a giant head crowned with a very official looking cap. In his grinning mouth is thrust a pipe and on the brim of the cap you can read "The Guardian."

How well I came to know that good guardian, and he always made me smile. But that day I had other things to think of.

On my return to the camp with the water, I had heard that a letter addressed to Lévi, from Loubens's father, had been sent down to the bottom of the shaft and had reached him. Soon we learnt what was in it, for from eleven hundred feet down Lévi read it out to the rest of us in a loud voice, made all the louder by the amplifiers up top.

Dear M. Lévi and members of the team,
     For several days now I have been following the work you are doing in the cave which holds the mortal remains of my beloved son. I do not have to tell you that I am with you in heart and thought.

In a few days, I trust, the body of Marcel will rest here at Mazères, in the cemetery of his native village.

If for any reason it is found that bringing the body to the surface might entail further loss of human life, I have complete confidence in you and leave the decision in your hands.

In the matter of legal formalities, should my consent in any point be needed, I give you, M. Lévi, full powers to act for me. But should my presence become absolutely necessary, I shall not fail to leave at once for Sainte-Engrâce.

However, I would ask you to spare me this last grievous journey, where I should be bound to be the object of all those curious eyes that follow this event. Spare me, I beg you, this last heartache.

When the body had been placed in the coffin, Lévi returned to the surface, where we questioned him with keen interest.

"It was hard work," he admitted. "Loubens's tomb was covered with a vast pile of stones and we had to clear away a good ton of them. Then we had to remove the large slabs which were placed over the body at the time of the accident in 1952, when we were sure that the cave would be Loubens's final resting place."

Lévi was not the type of man to show his feelings easily. He was cold by nature, and to sum him up I can only say that one admired rather than liked him. Casteret, who was not the leader, one liked. Still we accepted without question what Lévi said; he knew how to command men.

But when Lévi spoke of Loubens, his tone changed.

"He seemed to be sleeping. The cold had preserved his dead body marvellously, and he still weighed the same as when he was alive. We laid him to rest in a plastic bag, with a leather covering outside, and padded it all with cotton-wool. No, there will be nothing to fear on the way up."

He turned towards Vergnes, the cameraman, and in his normal voice he gave him the order.

" Get ready. It's your turn to go down now."

Then turning to me he went on:

" Father, when Vergnes comes up again, you will take his place."

It hardly seemed possible. How could I show my gratitude for this mark of confidence?

Perhaps I should explain that one does not go down a pot-hole as one does a cellar. A cellar has stairs where two men can pass. In a pot-hole there is only a cable. Our mission at Pierre Saint-Martin, moreover, ruled out any strange fancies. There was no time to lose. All our efforts had to be directed to bringing Marcel's body to the surface, and we had been warned from the outset: " Only those who have an important role to fulfil, will go down the hole."

I had an important role to fulfil, most certainly; to conse-crate a place where a Christian might perhaps lie for ever; the ascent, after all, had not yet been made. As a priest, I wished to ensure the Lord's part in the work. I felt that my prayers should be said as near as possible to where my friends were working. It was for this reason that I asked to go down to the bottom of the hole, with the sole object of celebrating the Holy Sacrament down there. To be sure, a Mass said at the edge of the *doline* would have been just as " profound " in its piety and sincerity as at the bottom of the shaft. But in that way, by bearing witness in that fashion, it seemed to me that I should encourage the whole team in the hard work that lay before them. Besides an accident was always possible.

How then to make that understood by people who had only the remotest links with Christianity? Many of the team had forgotten the path to the Church. Some had never even known it.

So it was with sincere gratitude that I welcomed Lévi's proposal. This man was a real leader. In the meantime, the village cabinet-maker at Licq-Atheray was at work on the coffin which was to bear Loubens to the cemetery in his native village.

MASS IS SAID IN THE BOWELS OF THE EARTH

When Vergnes came up again he was in poor shape and evidently the great depth did not agree with him. What was more he had dropped his camera while going down, and he now feared that the pictures he had taken would be ruined.

The harness was already being handed to me. I felt quite at ease. After all, I was hardly a novice, for only recently I had been down into caves and grottoes which, though they bore no resemblance to the Pierre Saint-Martin hole were full of serious difficulties. And, lastly, a final reason, I love adventure, and now it was my turn to see the world of which the others had so often spoken.

The first few yards plunged me into the darkness of night and though I began to drop without mishap I had a sudden feeling of anxiety, which I had not expected and which riled me. This feeling, experienced explorers were to tell me later, was quite natural. A good spelaeologist is not a daredevil; he is the sort of man who is always aware of danger and has a proper fear of it. Every normal man must go through this phase. Then I began to wonder how fast I was going down. Twenty feet a minute? Or forty? The cable would, of course, be unwound at whatever speed one liked. My estimate was that I was gliding down at the speed of a tortoise, which was a good sign and showed that I was already getting used to it.

Presently, I called up over my microphone:

"It's all going fine. Make it faster."

I liked the increase in speed. My thoughts no longer had time to dwell on idiotic details like: "Suppose the cable breaks?" After all, my position was exactly like that of someone dangling in space a thousand feet up—the height of the Eiffel Tower. "A loose stone could kill me!" "The winch might have a breakdown and then I should have to hang in the darkness for Heaven knows how long!" No, I had to be content with watching the sweating stone walls of the shaft and with keeping my legs clear to avoid any serious injury. Once the chimney grew wider, all I could do was keep on gliding as there was literally nothing to see but a kind of velvety darkness. The haze was thick and the light from the lamp on the front of my helmet hardly pierced it.

At point 700 I stopped. The depth marker here had been dislodged, and Quéffelec had asked me to stop and replace it. As soon as this was done, and after a last exchange of information with the surface, I went on my way again down into the Salle Lépineux; that is to say, into the part of the shaft where the walls suddenly widen and leave you hanging in an utter void.

Slowly the cable began to revolve and then to turn faster and faster, and this added to the water that had poured down me ever since point 700 soon turned my descent into an agony. It was then, when there was nothing I could do about it, that I remembered that it was just here that the accident had happened and the straps holding Loubens had given way.

I admit, without false shame, to having shuddered and to wishing that I were already at the bottom, standing alongside the others.

Where were they? I could neither see nor hear anything of them, for the noise of the falling water drowned all other sounds. Should I suddenly find myself at their side without even having realised that the descent was over and that this was the end of my journey?

I was still wondering about this when a bright light brought a sudden end to my fears. My arrival had, indeed, been noticed! Below me a torch was lighting up the cave. It was fantastic.

God, what a spectacle I beheld! All that my mind had conjured up paled into insignificance and vanished before the imposing work of Nature.

I was overwhelmed with wonder and awe. Around me rose the interior of a vast cathedral of rose-coloured granite, whose ordered architecture had been overthrown by the hand of a Titan. I forgot my fears, the icy douche, the presence of my comrades sixty feet below, some of whom had been there for days. And I gave thanks to the Creator.

Here I was at the bottom of the deepest known cave in the world. Until now that had meant nothing more to me than a rather empty phrase. But here, before this scene which was bound to restore spontaneously a sense of the divine even to the greatest unbeliever, how could any man remain unmoved?

Another vision began to rise before my eyes, a vision nurtured in the spirit. I saw myself celebrating Mass next morning. And for having granted me that supreme joy, I thanked Our Saviour from the bottom of my heart.

I was welcomed by Casteret and Delteil, who took me over to the bivouac where hot coffee was waiting.

"Where are the others?"

Where were Mairey, Mauer and Ballandreaux?

With the air of a conspirator Delteil mysteriously put a finger to his lips:

"Sst . . ." he said. "Not a word to anyone. . . . They are in Spain!"

"What? In Spain?"

Casteret explained.

"Delteil means *under* Spain. You can't expect a real spelaeologist to sit patiently doing nothing, until it is time to return to the surface. Time hangs heavy, and there may still be something left to discover down here. Not on the French side, of course, where everything is known, but on the other side."

"And?"

"I think it may well be something quite sensational. This Pierre Saint-Martin hole is literally inexhaustible."

He then went on to tell me that the Spanish branch opened on a vast hall, the Navarre cave, and that this had a passage that sloped upwards for about a hundred yards before opening out into other important caves, of which quite a small one was extremely rich in tree-like deposits of white calcspar.

"And inside," Casteret went on delightedly, " there are still more branches. Ballandreaux discovered a gigantic lateral cave which he christened 'Madeleine'. And then there was a fissure full of stalagmites and stalactites. I have never seen anything like them before and God knows I have seen plenty!"

"And beyond," Delteil chimed in, no longer able to contain his excitement, " the passage widened before stopping at a lake thirty feet long."

" Is that the end?"

" We don't think so. A strong breeze was blowing and the surface of the lake was ruffled at times by small waves. There must be an outlet . . . an outlet on the Arres d'Anie."

I was content, after resting and warming myself—there was a constant temperature down here of about forty degrees —to make for the caves which had already been explored, the Casteret, the Loubens, the Métro, etc. I did not go to the bottom to the famous La Verna cave at a depth of 1,388 feet, which is big enough to hold Notre Dame de Paris with ease and even the vast cathedral of Tournai in Belgium.

There was enough to occupy me in the nearby caves, which are so vast that you would easily become lost in them if the way was not marked. Red and green fluorescent bands on the rocks showed exactly what route to take. If you found yourself in front of a green line, all was well and the right track lay ahead of you. But if you came face to face with a red line, it meant " Halt! There's no way through here. Go back!"

Without these guidelines it would have been just like exploring the cave for the first time. The chaos of rubble surpassed anything one could imagine, and it is a fact that Casteret himself, the man who had explored more caves than anyone else, lost his way six times in one single cave.

It was that evening that I said my Mass, instead of the following morning as had been my previous intention. The reason was that I found myself with two Christians, and because the others—those who were exploring Spain—were agnostics. The conditions were ideal.

I wondered what I was to use for an altar on which to celebrate the Holy Sacrament. The container, perhaps, but

I thought that the medicine chest would be better. I wedged it as best I could on a pile of large stones, on the very spot where Marcel Loubens had died a lingering death two years before, and twenty yards from where his body now lay. " O Lord," I prayed before beginning the Sacrament, " if it is Thy will that his body be restored to his mother, let Thy will be done." Was it not the moment to say with Holy Church: *"De profundis* . . . out of the depths I cry to Thee, O my God "*?

What an unique Mass! I knew that there was activity at every point down the shaft and that nothing could interrupt it. At points 700 and 260, Lépineux, Labeyrie and Bidegain worked on, that all might be ready. Here, at the bottom, contact had to be maintained with the outside world and the life-line that trailed over the rubble had never to be lost from sight.

" I'll take care of it!"

It was Delteil who spoke. He was greatly moved by the preparations. At half past seven in the evening our first prayers rose to the vault above.

Casteret was my server, a true server in spirit and in deed, for he had to keep watch upon my altar, which was threatening every moment to fall. A little farther off, Delteil was praying with fervour, but every now and then he went over to the telephone and talked for a moment to the man on the winch, while still going on winding up the cable. Never again should I celebrate such a Mass in a setting that was so closely united to the Divine Sacrament.

I felt that we all three excelled ourselves. Nothing showed, of course, apart from the furtive tear which Delteil brushed away awkwardly with his finger. I wondered how we would appear to any chance observer. Three insignificant men, ill-clad, numb with cold, dirty, muddy, moving slowly round a makeshift altar, afraid that it would overbalance and keeping a careful eye on operations in the cave. In this vast cave we must look more like insects than human beings.

And yet . . . our souls were on fire. We were so far from our surroundings or if we sensed them at all it was because

WORKING IN THE SHAFT: *pitons* (*top*) were used to ensure the safety of men stationed on the ledges. The profile (seen in the lower photographs) is moored in position in the shaft, in the hope of guiding the container past obstructions.

Supplies for the 1954 expedition were dropped near Pierre Saint-Martin by parachute (*left*). Amongst them was the container (*right*) in which Loubens's coffin was placed before the ascent was made.

they had lost something of their material quality and become vast and luminous.

Lord, I thank Thee.

THE LAST HOURS

"Father . . . Father . . . Tell me . . . Is my wife there?"
And suddenly I was brought back to reality.

The storm was still raging at daybreak and we were all still gathered at the edge of the *doline* waiting for Bidegain to come up.

I looked at Marie. While I was talking to her husband about the happy days gone by, she had stayed close beside me, refusing to take any rest at all.

Now she shook her head.

I lied:

"No, José, she is not here."

"Ah! So much the better. I should be upset to know that she was on the edge of the *doline*. She might be worried. But if any of you see her, wish her many happy returns."

He gasped for breath, for, although he had stopped a long time at point 260, a halt would never be enough to restore his strength. That had been exhausted too long for him to recover easily.

"We are all with you, José."

How I wished that my voice had muscles to draw him up . . . but I could only keep saying:

"Rest a moment. Recover your breath."

After making the container fast on the platform, Lépineux had come up to the surface and had been followed by Mauer and Rossini. Only Bidegain now remained in the chimney, with the coffin and his utter exhaustion.

"José refused . . ." grumbled Lépineux gloomily. "I begged him to take my place and to come up right away. I was fresher than he was and could well have taken over from him for the last two hundred and sixty feet."

And he repeated:

MPSM 4

" But he refused."

Bidegain knew too well by that time how difficult the ascent was, and he trusted no one but himself. He felt as though he were part of the cable and the cylinder. And no one should succeed in separating him from it.

We at the surface could say no more. The last two sixty feet, as we all knew, offered endless difficulties. The bottleneck became narrower and began to spiral. We wondered how our weary giant would be able to get through.

" You should see his hands," said Lépineux. " They're no longer hands. Just dead flesh, swollen . . ."

And seizing the telephone he called down the shaft:

" José! Please . . . shall we throw you down another rope?"

But the boy from Pau summoned strength to reply:

" It's not worth the trouble. It's going better now."

And he promptly proved it by bounding fifteen feet. I wondered where he found the energy.

From Lépineux's description we could easily picture how Bidegain was progressing.

" Another six inches. He slips between the coffin and the rock. A struggle, stone by stone. He is leaning against the wall. Pulls on the chains. Pushes the container with his foot. And another six inches . . ."

We listened in a kind of stupor while work went on at the winch, and orders were given just the same.

By now morning was well advanced, a grey morning in which the surrounding mountains seemed to pierce the mist with heart-rending slowness.

Someone asked for the first time:

" When will all this be over?"

Lévi was there. He moved his head sharply.

" When? By midday for certain."

How far away that seemed.

Snow began to fall again in gusts, and the reporters, photographers and newsreel men who flocked round the *doline,* cast long dark shadows. There were several onlookers from Licq as well.

The question was repeated, this time more urgently:
"But when?"
And was followed by:
"How far down is he?"
By midday he had only sixty feet left to climb. But the way he gasped for breath, exaggerated by the amplifier, told us better than any words how exhausted José Bidegain was. He was now coming up only an inch at a time. For ten, sometimes fifteen seconds, the winch would work and stop again.

And then, and then . . .
"Here he is!"
Lépineux leaning over the narrow opening brought us the good news at last!

It was almost unbelievable! Was it really true that Bidegain was nearing the surface, bringing with him the cylinder containing Loubens's body?

There were only a few feet left to go, and then Bidegain appeared, his face unrecognisable.
"Quick! Quick! A rope! Throw me a rope!"
It was Lépineux who threw the rope and Bidegain was hauled up like a parcel and when at last he stood on the top he collapsed in the mud, his body racked with sobbing, and fainted.

The cameras clicked and whirred.

But that left me unmoved. I was overwhelmed with gladness, for I knew that we had just relived in all their force those words of the Master: "Love one another, even as I have loved you."

Chapter Three

1953

FRONTIER STONE 261

PIERRE SAINT-MARTIN, to parody the title of a book that had its hour of fame, is much more than Pierre Saint-Martin. By that I mean that the hole and its exploration are one thing; its folklore and, above all, its politics are quite a different matter. We were brought face to face with this in 1953 and from the very first day.

As soon as I arrived at Licq-Atheray at the beginning of August and went to the Hôtel des Touristes, where I had not stayed before, being a raw recruit to spelaeology, I noticed an unmistakable air of excitement. Everybody was on edge and talking a great deal.

"Look here," said one man, sitting with a glass of red wine in front of him. " They are now trying to prevent access to the hole. They've even got the impudence to send carabineers up to watch the approaches. They can't get away with that!"

"They," be it said, were the Spanish Government.

There had been a little friction in previous years, without any serious situation developing. This time, however, things seemed to be taking a more alarming turn.

There was already a substantial number of us at Licq-Atheray. The whole team was there, in fact, with equipment and baggage, rich in first-class material and perfectly organised. The French gendarmerie and army were co-

operating with us, and the airmen at the base at Pau had
arranged to drop provisions to us by parachute, over and
above all that the mules and we ourselves could carry. Needless to say, an expedition of this kind cost a great deal of
money.

Were "they" then, abruptly, without a note of warning,
going to use armed force to stop us going down to the
bottom of the Lépineux hole, getting on with the exploration, and paying our respects to Marcel Loubens's grave?

What right had they?

"The hole is French, unquestionably French!" was the
general cry. "The entrance is French and the underground
caves stretch out towards Sainte-Engrâce, that is to say,
towards France. The Spaniards have nothing to do with it."

On the other side of the Pyrenees, of course, the cry was
different.

"The Pierre Saint-Martin hole is Spanish! The frontier
posts show the line of demarcation clearly. Even if the
underground caves actually lead towards France, the
entrance to the shaft itself is on our soil."

Who was right? As usual in this kind of dispute—everybody and nobody. For these disputes do not arise out of
nothing—their real causes lie in the past, in traditions and in
the absence of them as well.

The story goes that some time in the last century, French
and Spanish shepherds who had foregathered on the Pierre
Saint-Martin ridge to celebrate the *Junta de Roncal*—an
ancient ceremony that has been observed since 1375—
decided on the spur of the moment, for a wager, to move
frontier stone 261 some four hundred yards back into French
territory. The shepherds told me that this was only just
another legend.

Consequently, the real frontier, the one which had been
fixed on 2 December 1856 as a result of a treaty signed
between Spain and the France of Napoleon III, and which
follows frontier stones 260, 261, 262, etc., was by now quite
difficult to define.

Old land registers were ransacked, journalists crossed

swords, historians were busy collecting all the documents they could find to sustain their theories, whatever these might be.

Some said: "If you follow an imaginary line from one stone to the next, taking the present position of the frontier stones, you will find that the entrance is on Spanish soil."[1]

But the same people, and others too, added: "If, on the other hand, you follow the mule track and take into account the fact that the treaty of 1856 granted France fifty additional acres, then there is no doubt about it at all, the entry to the hole is in France."

But none of this mattered to us. However subtle the arguments, they did not alter our position in the slightest. We were ready with our mules and our baggage, and we knew that up on the ridge armed carabineers were standing guard.

All eyes turned to Lévi, the leader of the expedition. It was for him to decide.

Lévi took the whole thing with composure, without getting ruffled, very sure of himself and very much the leader.

"There is no valid reason why we should interrupt the final preparations. We will, therefore, go up to the Pierre Saint-Martin. Let us act first and talk after."

This, too, was our opinion. All the same, to hear it expressed with such force and clarity by the man who bore the whole responsibility for the success of the expedition, spurred us on like the lash of a whip.

Even the rain did not damp our enthusiasm, for in the meantime it had begun to pour. I still remember those reporters, beautifully turned out but unwary, who were suddenly turned into scarecrows, drenched to the bone, pitiable objects toiling up the track, their eyes scanning the bare mountain for the shelter that was nowhere to be found.

Imagine climbing six thousand feet up a mountain dressed

---

[1] The famous stone 261, which some reporters claimed had disappeared, I myself found with the help of the shepherds not far from the *doline*. When haziness or jingoism appear truth is hard to establish.

for a Press conference! The best part about it was that, for
all that, there was to be a Press conference here, and something even better than a Press conference, a reconciliation
dinner in the big official tent, which we have called ever
since the " Panmunjom " tent, for at the time, as it happened,
Korea was very much in the news while the difficult negotia-
tions for putting an end to the conflict dragged on there
eternally.

With us, however, everything was settled in five days.

On 5 August, to be precise, the prefect of Pau and the
Governor of Navarre climbed, probably for the first time in
their lives, to the Pierre Saint-Martin ridge. At all costs this
smouldering dispute had to be settled.

When we arrived at this arid spot, which before Loubens's
death had attracted no attention whatsoever, except among
a few shepherds who were established there for the summer
in picturesque stone shacks, we found eight carabineers
waiting for us. To tell the truth, they had no liking at all for
being there, for they were wet through and furious at having
had to leave their barracks. Some of the brightest of them
had unearthed an old umbrella and were huddling under its
dripping cover.

We were almost sorry for them, but they looked at us as
though we were dogs.

The Madrid Government had forwarded its conditions;
the exploration of the hole might take place :

1. If the French Government officially recognised that
the entrance really lay inside the Spanish frontier.

2. If the expedition included at least three Spanish
spelaeologists.

3. If it were given the title of " The Franco-Spanish
Scientific Expedition."

We agreed—without agreeing.

Lévi sent a masterly reply :

" I could wish nothing better than to have some Spaniards
with us. The presence of several more competent men at

Pierre Saint-Martin could not fail to be of the greatest benefit to us. Whether the expedition should be called ' Franco-
Spanish,' or even ' Franco-Belgo-Italo-Anglo-Spanish,' as
spelaeologists from all those countries are taking part, is of
no importance. A name has never altered facts. But that we
should acknowledge that the entrance to the caves lies in
Spain is something that we cannot agree to, for it is a point
on which not one of us here is qualified to give a serious
opinion. I am willing to write to Paris, but you will realise
that ministers cannot reach decisions in twenty-four hours
nor even in fifteen days, and at the end of that time we ourselves shall be far away."

At the end of four days Madrid seemed to understand.

That was why on 5 August, at an altitude of six thousand
feet, in surroundings that were rich only in stones, bitter
herbs, sheep and wind, but that possessed a pot-hole more
than a thousand feet deep, certain personages representing
the two governments found themselves gathered round a
table to celebrate.

" Look," Professor Llopis fired at me (he was one of the
three Spanish spelaeologists who had joined our team), " the
Pierre Saint-Martin ridge has become so important a place
that it ought to be made an international zone. A zone of
which I, of course, should be the Governor and you, my dear
Father, the Bishop. . . ."

He had had a few drinks, the good professor, and it was
the moment to be expansive. We were all laughing round the
table, happy to think that a provisional solution had been
found; and even the carabineers, who had appeared so surly
at our first meeting, were rapidly changing into helpful
friends.

The dispute being settled, we wondered why it was that
the Spaniards attached so much importance to our expedition, which despite the publicity surrounding it was of no
importance at all to anyone except its members.

Officially we knew no reason why, the Madrid Government having treated the subject with the greatest discretion.
But an unofficial rumour was going round that it was not a

question of prestige, nor a matter of who owned a few acres
of ground; it was, in fact, an economic problem.

It seemed likely that France, after our explorations and
discoveries, would proceed to exploit the underground water
power and turn it to her own exclusive profit—as was her
right—whereas it could also be of benefit to the Spanish
economy.

But that evening in the Panmunjom tent there was no
question of that sort. Good humour reigned undisturbed,
for we were all thinking of the shaft down which Lépineux
would descend at dawn next day to make a hasty recon-
naisance.

Well before nightfall I returned to the shepherd's hut in
which I was lodged and there, listening to the wind, I
dreamed for long hours of the adventure that was beginning.

TAZIEFF AT THE COLLEGE

For me it was the start of an exhilarating adventure.

I wonder when I first said to myself that I *had* to go with
the Pierre Saint-Martin expedition. Was it before Loubens's
tragic death, or was it at that very moment, when my priest's
heart could not endure the thought that there was no
spiritual healer among those who were risking their lives at
each descent, while the healers of bodily ills were excel-
lently represented there by Dr Mairey?

It does not matter as it was all decided by an event banal
enough in itself.

That year I was still a professor at the college at Soignies.
I heard one day that Haroun Tazieff, the explorer of vol-
canoes, who lived in Brussels when not away in Africa or
elsewhere, was going to visit us to give a lecture on the
famous Pierre Saint-Martin pot-hole.

Tazieff . . . Tazieff . . . who had taken part in the first
expedition, and who had held young Loubens in his arms as
he lay dying. I knew what I had to do, and as soon as the

last applause died away I walked over to the lecturer and opened my heart.

"I very much want to go down the hole with you. A priest would not be unwelcome would he?"

"I don't think so," Tazieff replied; and added: "It is not for me to make any decision, as I am not the leader. You should know, of course, that there is a flood of applications. Have you, by the way, had any experience of underground exploration?"

It happened that I had. I had often visited the Meuse caves with some of my students.

"Perfect," said Tazieff. "Well, write to Casteret and go and see Lévi in Paris. After all, the final decision is his. I will let him know of your intention."

I realised that it would not be easy, for the chief need below ground was for professional spelaeologists, or at least for young men trained in all the complicated work which the very nature of caving made essential, a mixture of mountaineering and underwater exploration, mountaineers and frogmen combined, in fact.

Still, without giving up hope I wrote to Casteret and to Lévi; and then I went to see Lévi in Paris.

"We will write to you."

That was all the leader of the expedition would promise. *In principle* I was accepted, not as a member of the caving team proper, but merely as one of the group in charge of surface operations.

"*In principle*," insisted Lévi. "Someone may change his mind at the last moment. That is always possible. But don't be angry with me, if you have still heard nothing by June."

The months went by. Spring lengthened into summer and I began to have doubts. But I was wrong. For in June, as Levi had promised, came a letter telling me that all was going well.

And then, at the end of July, as I was having another fit of depression, a telegram arrived from France.

"Are you coming, Father? We are expecting you."

Several days later, after an inordinate amount of hitch-

hiking, I reached Bayonne. From there on to Licq-Atheray,
I found that transport was easy. All those spelaeologists
whom I knew by name, from having read about them in the
papers, suddenly became real people with faces, voices and
shapes. At first the atmosphere was a little constrained, but
soon there was a joke, a glass of wine and some job to do
together to make the recruit feel himself accepted as one of
the team.

The formal " you " and the set phrases prepared before-
hand were discarded, and I was soon saying " thou " and
" thee " to Norbert Casteret, Lévi, Bidegain, Quéffelec,
Treuthard, Lépineux and the Lyons scouts.

" Up there, Father, we shall entrust you with an important
mission."

It was Lévi speaking. My heart was beating faster. Con-
found it.

" You are charged with the care of our stomachs. Cook
and water-carrier, how will that suit you?"

Well, there was nothing to be said. They could not be
expected to trust me with the winch. So I had to put a good
face on it and laugh.

" Yes, that will suit me very well. I'll try not to poison you.
And, if any of you get ulcers, well, there's always the
doctor!"

Though I had left home with the fixed idea of never
leaving the shaft, reducing in my mind the whole world of
Pierre Saint-Martin to the pot-hole itself, I accepted the post
of maid-of-all-work with good grace but without enthusiasm.
I was, however, about to discover, up on the top of the
mountain, in some small way as a result of my lowly tasks,
a universe strangely remote from everything, a universe of
calm, a life of peace, a world two steps from heaven; the
world of the summertime shepherds and their *cayollards*.

The shepherds' names were Mazéris, Bigué, Tham-Tham,
Cot-de-la-Motte—names of Basque or Béarn origin. There
were six of them up there on that vast broken plateau, shut
in between the peaks of Soum de Lèche and Anie.

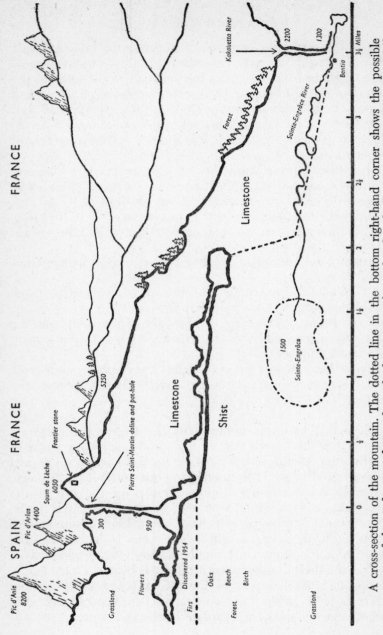

A cross-section of the mountain. The dotted line in the bottom right-hand corner shows the possible course of the underground river from the last point to be explored in the La Verna cave up to its outfall at Bentia.

On the first of May the shepherds leave the village in the valley and move upwards stage by stage, as the snow and the cold retreat before them. They do not come down again until 15 September, having watched their flocks on these alpine pastures of France and Spain as they had contracted to do. For four months they live there with their sheep, between two and three hundred in the care of each man, and they sleep in a sort of hut, called a *cayollard*, open to the wind and rain.

In days gone by these shepherds' forefathers were attacked by the Spaniards, on whom they inflicted a bloody defeat; and out of the agreement that was made afterwards was perhaps born this controversy over frontier stone 261.

In the course of a fortnight I got to know the shepherds. There was a former magistrate among them, a shepherd called Lagrave, who was seventy years old and had retired from his profession. He was in no way different from his humbler companions, and came up every year with his sheep and a few young pigs. We used to go, from time to time, to his hut for shelter and rest, and to steady our nerves, which can trouble the strongest characters.

I have often seen Lagrave at seven in the evening counting his sheep with his long crook. He did it very quickly and not a sheep escaped him. If an animal was missing he set out to search for it. One evening he came back with a lamb draped round his neck, reminding me of the Good Shepherd. With his fervent faith and exemplary life he was, indeed, rather like Him.

"Ha!" he said. "This youngster wanted to do like M. Sequin's goat!" He was a man of letters, this magistrate turned shepherd.

Even when sudden drama came to the ridge he retained a calm that is unknown among townspeople. It is at such times that the great and simple virtues are called forth— among men and among animals, too. On the second evening I spent with him he told me the story of Sentola's hut.

"The shepherd had gone off, leaving his flock alone with the sheepdog. Well, one of the sheep had fallen sick and was dying. Warned by instinct the dog kept watch by it.

" An hour later thirty vultures, some of them with wings eight feet wide, circled overhead with raucous cries. I was watching from a distance, bitterly regretting that I had no gun to bring one of them down. One shot into their midst would have been enough. The dog, lying by the dead sheep, never stirred, but waited for the attack.

" The vultures sensed the situation. Quickly they stopped circling and alighted in a circle round the faithful dog, about twenty yards away to avoid being bitten. Then, like skilled tacticians, they began to move forward—you might almost think that one of them had given the word of command—closing the circle inch by inch. The battle was on . . .

" There was no sound at first, only the most sinister silence. The dog knew what he had to do, and that to threaten action was not enough. Curling back his lips, he growled and stood erect. Slowly he advanced a paw. The vultures understood, and those in front of him retreated, leaving it to the others behind him to take advantage of his being occupied in front and move forward to gain as much ground as they could. For a time the dog chased them. He spared no effort. He attacked first to the right, then turned about to attack on the left, trying to prevent the circle from narrowing still further.

" The vultures in front of him would jump grotesquely back a few yards, while others would move nearer the carcase with the same ugly action. It was an exhausting battle, a sickening battle of cowards against a solitary brave spirit, a battle where it was impossible to come to grips, where weariness alone would decide the victory. It lasted two hours, two long hours, in the course of which I could sometimes hear the dog howling.

" When he was near the end of his strength, the dog withdrew a few paces, slavering and trembling all over, and lay down. This was the signal for a general scramble. Taking no notice now of their enemy, the vultures fell upon the dead sheep, ripping open its belly, literally emptying the carcass and, having first devoured the entrails, left nothing at the finish but a skeleton cleaned to the bone. Then, gorged, they took flight, heavily and in silence.

"After a while the shepherds returned and the dog, its eyes large and sad, fawned on one of them. Instead of yelping at him reproachfully in anger or shame, his look only seemed to say: 'Do not blame me! I did what I could!'"

I spent some delightful hours with Lagrave listening to his stories, but we did not talk all the time we were together. In such a setting silence took on a rare quality. These shepherds were in no sense out of touch with the world, but they were used to spending their days in almost complete silence, making the communion of heart and soul with the mountain world. Wrapped in their goat-skins they leaned on their long crooks and watched the flight of the eagle and the vulture in the deep ravine, while the sheepdog watched over the flock and chased the unwary away from holes in the ground.

Living in a world of calm amid the beauties of Nature, they knew nothing of the nervous excitement of modern life. They were incapable of the sensational, their simplicity was too great. In short, they did but do their duty, and for this reason perhaps they have been rather ignored by the Press. God Himself has never abandoned them, but has loaded them with favours; eternal snows without end, to the limit of their vision, the impressive sea of clouds, magnificent and intensely calm; perpetual silence all around and on some evenings sunsets with unforgettable colours; the flight of the birds of prey, becoming invisible as they rise towards the high peaks. And down there below, in the valley a few miles away, the tiny village of Sainte-Engrâce, microscopic, barely visible, from where from time to time rose the prayers of their brothers towards the " Kingdom of the Skies " to which the shepherds themselves seemed already to belong. Witnesses, relics, some say, of ancestral traditions several thousand years old, the shepherds could not be unaware of the eternal Truth. I would claim that it lies there before them. They have only to raise their eyes to discover God and His mystery, while in our modern towns with their enveloping tentacles we are chained and ensnared by the materialism of Antichrist.

One evening I saw Lagrave return to his hut with sadness in his eyes. He had gone to search for a lost sheep. I had said to him : " Don't worry. You will find it, as before, with a slightly injured foot; and you will end by bringing it home round your neck." But this time he returned alone without the animal.

It was not until just before lying down for the night that he murmured :

" Oh! It's nothing. She will spend the night in the open between two rocks. She must have hurt her foot more severely this time."

They have courage, these shepherds of Pierre Saint-Martin, and are true masters of this desolate and arid high plateau. I wonder what we should have done without them, what we should have become if they had not been there. They gave us shelter at night; they allowed us to store cumbersome and costly gear in their huts, they watched over our cases of food and our papers; they gave us hot coffee when we returned exhausted. And they shared their water with us, so scarce and precious because it has to be carried up over four thousand feet from the springs in the forest below.

On 14 August, the anniversary of Loubens's death, I celebrated Mass near the hole on a table brought by the shepherds. All of them were present, as well as the members of our team, whether believers or unbelievers. It was a true Mass of all Nature, a Mass for all the world, such as St Francis of Assissi would have loved. A dog lay down at my feet, under the rustic altar, and stayed there throughout the Holy Sacrament.

WHO WE ARE

We now know that the great year for Pierre Saint-Martin was not 1952, the year of Loubens's death, nor 1954, the year of the recovery of his body, but 1953. In that year teams A, B and C, formed from the most experienced members of the group of thirty men who composed the expedition and shared the work, succeeded in reaching the last of the caves, 2,400 feet below ground. A world record had been broken.

The operation began on 7 August with the descent of Norbert Casteret. Lépineux had gone down before for a preliminary " chimney sweeping," but he had stopped at the 260-foot ledge. By 19 August the year's exploring was over. For twelve days a handful of men had lived a life of darkness, danger and exhaustion, with moments of hope and dejection, with moments, too, of fear.

Here are the names of these men with a little about each of them :

Norbert Casteret: Celebrated his fifty-sixth birthday six hundred feet underground, dangling on the end of a rope. The sparking plugs in the winch had sooted up and the cable could not be raised or lowered. That was on 19 August. Norbert Casteret is a professional spelaeologist who has explored more caves and holes than anyone else, but remains modest and silent about his exploits. Needless to say, everyone likes him.

Georges Lépineux: The hole was named after him for the simple reason that he was the first to discover it and the first to go down it. In civil life he is a jeweller at Bagnères-de-Bigorre. This evidently allows him some leisure, for not content with exploring caves in the Pyrenees each summer, he has taken part in major explorations. In 1952 he was a member of Liotard's South Polar expedition to Adélie Land.

Robert J. Lévi: Works in Paris as a business consultant, and was therefore bound to be chosen automatically as the leader of the expedition to Pierre Saint-Martin. He carried out his delicate task with infinite diplomacy and authority, and was respected and admired by all.

André Mairey: A doctor from Lures, and the expedition's medical officer. Had little use for reporters. To one of their number, who had injured a knee and asked him to look at it, he once replied frigidly: "I am the spelaeologists' doctor, not the reporters!" For all that, very courageous and unsparing of himself. Left no stone unturned to save Loubens. One of the most engaging personalities of the group.

Jacques Théodor: Director of a synthetic textiles laboratory at Ghent. An old hand at Pierre Saint-Martin and a specialist in water exploration, both by rubber canoe and in frogman's kit. Burst an ear-drum as the result of training too violently. Explored (with the Lyons scouts) the Gave *siphons* in the Sainte-Engrâce valley. Was later engaged in exploring the caves at Han in Belgium, and the underground course of the Lesse, then unknown, for a distance of more than a mile.

The Lyons Scouts: The Ballandreaux brothers, the Epelly brothers and Letrône. Were exploring a hole near Pierre Saint-Martin at the time of the accident to Loubens. Went down the shaft with rope ladders, work at which they were past masters. In their honour the last and deepest cave in the system, as well as the most impressive, was named the "La Verna" cave, after the name of their group.

Jacques Ertaud: Professional cameraman. Specialist in underwater diving. Had climbed some of the highest mountains before taking to going down the deepest caves. At Pierre Saint-Martin in 1951 and 1953. The hardiest of spelaeologists. In order to make a good film, stayed ten days underground and returned to the surface in remarkably fine physical condition.

José Bidegain: Manufacturer at Pau. Like Loubens, a pupil of Casteret. But never knew Loubens. Became famous in 1954, after his exploit in bringing up Loubens's body. His knowledge of Spanish made him the "diplomat" of the expedition. Was often our intermediary with the carabineers and the Spanish authorities.

Cotentin Quéffelec: Engineer, specialising in lifting gear. Built the winch and the "auto-lift," thanks to which it was possible to bring the coffin up. Never went down the shaft.

Louis Delteil: Carpenter at Foix. Hardened spelaeologist. Friend of Loubens and Casteret. Took the coffin down the shaft. The type of craftsman who likes a job well done.

Beppo Occhialini : Italian spelaeologist of standing. Shared in most of the Pierre Saint-Martin explorations. Specialist in nuclear physics; unsuccessful candidate for the Nobel prize.

Jean Janssens: An engineer at the Peugeot factory. Worked the first pedal-winch, which Cosyns had designed and which made it possible for Lépineux to go down to the bottom of the shaft in 1951. Also supplied the parts for the second winch used in 1952 and made the steel cross-bar and clamps.

Pierre Louis : Works Manager at the Peugeot factory for twenty years. It was really he who made the winch which Cosyns had designed. Also suggested some modifications which very much improved the working of Quéffelec's winch. A hard worker.

The Spaniards : Professor Llopis Llado, Xaime Assens, Jésus Eloséguy, Miguel de Ondarra, and Fernando Termes. Put in an appearance. Owing to an attack of claustrophobia, Assens had to be brought back to the surface with all speed.

Jacques Attout : " Padre " of the 1953 and 1954 expeditions. Celebrated Mass at the bottom of the shaft. Formerly Professor at the college at Soignies. Vicar at Quaregnon, in the Borinage district of Belgium.

In 1953 three spelaeologists of former years were unable to rejoin us : *Haroun Tazieff*, then acting as a reporter in Kenya, *Jacques Labeyrie*, an atomic scientist engaged on writing a thesis, and *Max Cosyns*, the inventor of the first pedal winch.

IN SPAIN DEATH IS NOT GREEDY

Acute fear, panic fear, seized Norbert Casteret. Mairey, the doctor, had just fallen heavily to the foot of a wall of crumbling schist and water was already beginning to cover his unconscious body. In spite of his years of experience, Casteret for a time failed to realise the critical nature of the

MPSM 5*

situation. He lost his head for a minute or two, and took a photograph of the injured man!

Being the first to come down with the doctor, he had proposed that they should explore in a direction that—up to then—had remained virgin ground: the Spanish side. And Mairey had agreed.

The difficulties were serious. The two men suddenly found themselves involved in a regular chaos of rocks of all shapes and sizes, where a lizard would certainly have been more at home than a man. All the same, despite this earthquake-ridden ground, they soon found the stream again, and this Ariadne's thread of Pierre Saint-Martin helped the explorers to make real progress towards the Pic d'Anie.

Suddenly the waterfall appeared in front of them. It might have been fifteen feet high; certainly no impassable barrier, but dangerous because of the nature of the rock.

Casteret went first and succeeded in going down the wall without mishap.

Then it was Mairey's turn.

He grasped a jutting piece of schist. The stone was rotten, and giving way under his weight it took the unfortunate doctor with it. Falling the full height of the waterfall and landing on his back, he might have been seriously injured.

Recovering his wits Casteret seized the doctor under the armpits to drag his body out of the water. Mairey was heavy and inert; and blood flowed freely from a wide curving cut on his brow.

" *Agur Maria Gracias bethia !*" exclaimed Casteret, unthinkingly beginning an *Ave Maria* in the Basque language. " How shall I get him back to camp if he is seriously injured?"

It was difficult enough for an active man, for he had to crawl and at the same time take care not to disturb ground which might easily give way under his weight; but for someone in charge of a helpless casualty it was impossible.

Was there to be a second version of the Loubens's drama?

Mairey became heavier and heavier, and Casteret could

no longer hear him breathing. The flow of blood made the pallor of his face seem even more alarming, and when a violent shudder shook his body from head to foot, one single thought flashed through Casteret's brain:

" It's all over . . . he's dying in my arms!"

At that moment Mairey opened his eyes, evidently having no wish to play such a dirty trick on his companion.

" What's going on here?" Mairey mumbled, half conscious.

Casteret gave a sigh of relief and began a voluble explanation of what had happened, but the victim appeared to be hardly listening.

The doctor was now seated on a stone, feeling his forehead; this he did with the greatest care, as if he were examining a scalp wound on a patient, and not at all as though it was himself that he was treating.

" I don't think there is any fracture," Mairey said at last, phlegmatically. And he started to get up. Casteret had quite a battle to make him stay quiet and to put on the temporary dressing that he had improvised.

The return to the camp was painful. But the first few moments inside the tent bordered on high comedy, for when the others there, including Janssens, the engineer, Ertaud, Treuthard and Ondarra, saw the bandage over Mairey's eye they exclaimed in alarm.

The doctor waved them aside, and refused to listen. Casteret knew very well that he was furious with himself about the accident, and that the only thing was to leave him alone. Taciturn and phlegmatic, Mairey rummaged in his instrument case; then, interrupting his companion, who was in the middle of explaining to the others what had happened. he asked wryly:

" Do any of you know how to put stitches in?"

No, no one knew.

" Well, has anyone got a mirror in his kit?"

Someone had, as it happened.

Then Mairey removed the dressing Casteret had given him, asked Janssens to hold his acetylene lamp close to him, and without a grimace or, as far as we could see, any sign of feeling, put three stitches into his own forehead in masterly fashion, just like a fakir.

This is no second-hand story. I saw the whole operation with my own eyes and could judge our doctor's sangfroid for myself. And Ertaud filmed the whole episode.

PARTY A GETS UNDER WAY

Party A was now complete. Consisting of seven men, Casteret, Mairey, Delteil, Ertaud, Janssens, Ondarra and Treuthard, its plan was to explore the caves into which Loubens had ventured alone the year before, a few hours before his death.

The camp was near his tomb, and every time a beam of light fell on the stones covering the body, the cross shone brightly. Casteret, who had been the first to come down the shaft, had found, not without emotion, that thanks to the cold everything was in a perfect state of preservation.

"It's just as though we had only left the cave an hour ago," he told Mairey, who had followed him down the shaft. "Tents, blankets, mess-tins, stoves, clothes, nothing has changed." This was, of course, because the temperature never rose above forty-five degrees.

On Monday, 10 August, the party set off in the direction of the Elizabeth Casteret cave. Their first action was to put forty pounds of fluorescein in the water in order to trace its course and eventually find it again on the mountainside.

The plan was to go as far as possible, and pitch an advanced camp for party B, who were to relieve party A at seven o'clock in the evening, the hour fixed by Lévi.

As long as party A were in the Casteret and Loubens caves, which were already known and explored, all went splendidly. No one upset the time-table which Lévi had laid down. Once they had passed the "Métro," the long gallery in which ten trains could have been driven abreast, unknown ground began. The idea seemed to give Treuthard wings, and he set off at a great pace.

No man had ever before set foot where he now trod. After Loubens's death Mairey and Tazieff had, it is true, ventured as far as this, but they had retraced their steps, exhausted by their recent sad experiences.

Impatience was soon gnawing at the doctor. Walking in silence near Ertaud and Janssens—the rear-guard was made up of Casteret, Delteil and the Spaniard—his thoughts went back to the year before and he could not bear that another should be the first to explore *his* unknown country. No, Treuthard would not stay the leader for long.

Mairey quickly passed to the offensive, and shot by Ertaud and Janssens, slipping like a monkey between the rocks and risking a fall at each step on the slippery stones.

"Hey, Doc!" someone shouted as he rushed by. But Mairey heard nothing. The tunnel stretched out before him and he hurried on to find out what it opened into. Was it a wall, the end of the hole, or another cave? Gone was the memory of his injury, of the discipline called for by Casteret, of the steady pace at the start. The fervour of discovery now engrossed him, as it had already gripped Treuthard.

Ertaud and Janssens had to run to catch up with him. Then it was the Spaniard's turn.

"Oh, well!" fumed Casteret, left alone with Delteil, "if they keep pushing on at this speed we shall lose sight of them!"

"That is obvious!"

Delteil agreed with some emphasis; with too much, perhaps. His answer seemed more of a censure on his companion's slowness, wise though it might be, than on the haste of the others.

A quarter of an hour later Casteret was alone.

"Absurd," he thought. "There's no sense in this craze for speed. It is nearly six o'clock. This is not the time—we have to turn back to the base camp in an hour."

And he decided to increase his pace.

"Well," he exclaimed when he rejoined the leading group, "you seem to have forgotten the real idea behind

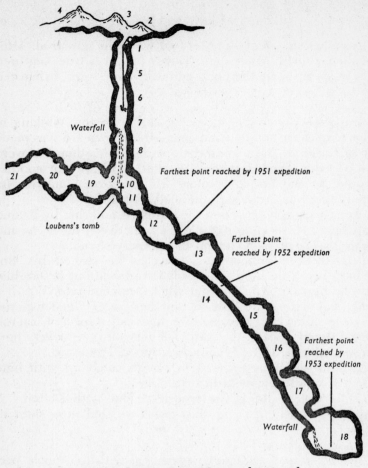

A cross-section of Pierre Saint-Martin, showing the progress made by the expeditions of 1951-54. It is not drawn to scale as the total length of the explored part of the pot-hole is over two miles while its depth is approximately two thousand four hundred feet.

1. Mouth of the pot-hole and winch. 2. Soum de Lèche. 3. Pic d'Arlas. 4. Pic d'Anie. 5-8. Main vertical shaft. 9. Lépineux cave. 10. Loubens's tomb. 11. Underground camp. 12. Elizabeth Casteret cave. 13. Loubens cave. 14. The Métro. 15. Quéffelec cave. 16. Adélie cave. 17. Chevalier cave. 18. La Verna cave. 19. La Navarre cave. 20. Vast ante-chamber. 21. Farthest point reached in 1954.

what we are doing—it is only a reconnaissance that we are making you remember, and the exploration itself is to be carried out by B party under Lépineux."

" Why?" someone retorted. " Since we are here first and everything is going well, I see little reason why we should give way to others."

" What about the plan we drew up? We all agreed on how the operation was to be divided between us, and we all accepted the same discipline."

But they behaved like madmen. Argumentative and self-willed, they were driven on by the fever of discovery to revolt and disobey Lévi's orders. Down there, at the bottom of the gallery, there must lie wonders, they had no doubt of it now, wonders that they would not give others the chance to discover.

" Casteret, let's push on!" one man begged. " Let's waste no more time! Come on!"

Casteret was not without the will to go on, but all the same his answer was :

" Let's not behave like spoilt children. Don't forget that Georges Lépineux is waiting for us, and he has a better right than any of us to be the first to explore whatever lies ahead. It's his hole we are in, you know, and he who discovered the opening and the first caves. It would be a dirty trick to rob him of his reward."

This time no one said a word.

" Come on," said Casteret. " Let's do the right thing, and keep going till seven o'clock, but not as though all we were trying to do was beat a speed record. Make a careful examination of the terrain as you go."

The moment of madness passed, and the hour of revolt never struck. The party regrouped round their leader, and went on exploring the " Métro " in a more sensible way.

The gallery soon began to widen, and suddenly their lamps flashed against a vast wall, which at first sight seemed impassable. This was certainly the end of the " Métro," and perhaps of the whole series of caves.

It was ten minutes to seven!

" No," murmured Treuthard, " we can't . . . we can't
turn back here."

Things began to look better as they explored the wall more
carefully with their lamps; it was the height of a six-storey
building and its vast overhang made it difficult to scale. The
stream disappeared underneath it and gave no clue of the
best route to follow.

They all looked at Casteret.

" Treuthard is right," he said slowly. " We must see what
there is behind this wall. . . . If there is anything."

The climb began at once. Casteret tried all the tricks he
knew but they soon proved useless. Halfway up he was
stopped and could find no way on. Mairey and Delteil pre-
ferred not to leave the stream, but in following it they
reached a *siphon*, which they were not equipped to pass.

It was Treuthard, the ebullient Treuthard, who found the
joint in the armour. Having climbed up the wall face on
the right, he started shouting from the top :

" I've found it! Come this way! "

A few minutes later the party were all up beside him.
They had slipped two or three times in the clay, which had
not improved the appearance of their clothes, but in the final
count all obstacles had been overcome.

Their lamps shone into the new unknown, and so vast
was the cave that opened up beyond the " Great Barrier "
that their beams did not reach the far walls.

There was a long silence.

Then someone exclaimed, awestruck :

" It does go on, then! "

Yes! It certainly went on.

Reluctantly, party A retraced its steps. It had delayed
long enough.

" Lépineux has all the luck! " grumbled Janssens. " Still,
I am satisfied. We have had our share of excitement."

And presently all their hardships, cold, stiffness, falls and
duckings in icy water, vanished in the elation of this day
lived in the night of underground discovery.

PARTY B's ACHIEVEMENT

Anyone who went down the Pierre Saint-Martin shaft had to be attached to the cable by a harness. This was an essential piece of equipment and when the team arrived at the beginning of August it had two. When exploration began there were still no more.

This was not due to lack of funds or to poor organisation, for in a matter like that Lévi was not likely to be found at fault. It was entirely due to a strike and to the fact that the extra harnesses despatched to Licq-Atheray by rail were held up somewhere or other. The strike made the ascent and descent of the thousand-foot shaft more difficult than it would have been in ordinary circumstances, for the lack of equipment meant that descents were fewer and slower.

Party B, consisting of Lépineux, Théodor and Epelly, was augmented by Ballandreaux and Letrône, who were to make topographical surveys. Ertaud, who belonged to party A, stayed on down at the bottom, at the entrance to the Lépineux cave, as he still had some details to film.

It took the three men four hours to reach the foot of the "Great Barrier," which rose massive and imposing some thousand yards beyond the foot of the main shaft. They scaled it without difficulty, being no doubt the most agile members of the team, though they were also helped by Treuthard's description of the best route.

They lost no time in plunging into the new cave, which they christened "Quéffelec cave," in honour of the engineer whose winch had been of such assistance in getting them so far.

The stream turned suddenly into a deep lake, and beyond that the vaulted roof dropped disturbingly. They had by now crossed the length of the Quéffelec cave and their next task was to discover what they would be faced with in the caves to come.

"This is not going to be so good," said Epelly, who had now to stoop as he walked. He was right, because the roof sloped down to the level of the water and there was only one way of passing the *siphon*—to undress (in a temperature of forty degrees, if you please) and dive in and swim underwater.

"Just a minute!" said Lépineux. "Perhaps there's another way."

After several attempts that led nowhere, he at last found an entry to a small lateral gallery which was quite dry and where the stream evidently only overflowed in flood time.

He went in, and came back a few minutes later.

"Come on, boys! This is the way. It's not good enough to risk on a bicycle, but it's a proper boulevard for people like us."

The "boulevard" soon brought the three men back alongside the watercourse, after which their route led across a very nasty ledge, narrow and slippery, along which they had to walk bent completely double, the roof being scarcely a yard above the water.

"Off packs!" ordered Lépineux, telling his team to pass them through by rope.

The route then became rather more civilised and the last stages provided no further hindrance.

"Good God!" exclaimed Epelly, as they reached the end of it. "Where are we?"

They could see nothing. The gallery opened out on pitchy darkness, and its walls disappeared into an icy void depriving the explorers of any sort of landmark.

Lépineux then lit a powerful magnesium flare.

A single cry of admiration came from all three. A vast, amazing cave, surpassing in size and splendour all that they had so far seen, larger than the Casteret and Loubens caves combined, more imposing than the Quéffelec and its annex the Adèlie, lay before them like a great vessel of stone plunging forward in the waves. They were spellbound. Gripped by excitement, feverishly, with the agility of animals used to virgin forests, they rushed forward jumping from rock to rock, striding over obstacles and avoiding impassable places as though by instinct; and eventually, breathless and bathed in sweat, but enchanted, they reached the far end of this cave, which they promptly decided to christen " Chevalier cave."

Pierre Chevalier was a noted spelaeologist, who at that time held the world's record for the deepest underground penetration, won in the Dauphiné, where he had reached a depth of 2,158 feet, while exploring the Trou du Glaz.

" What do you say?" queried Lépineux, opening and passing round a flask of rum. " Do you think we are lower than Chevalier?"

" I should be surprised if we were," replied Théodor. " We cannot be far off, but as for beating his record—no, that's impossible."

" Nonsense!" murmured Epelly. " Letrône and Ballandreaux will soon be here with their levels, and then we shall know exactly the depth at which we are drinking this excellent rum!"

After the Chevalier cave, there came another, its floor so uneven that progress was slow. But B party was carried away by enthusiasm and seemed to have wings. Lépineux, Théodor and Epelly would have been very surprised if they had been told that they were exhausted, or at the end of their strength. They seemed unconscious of how tired they were; wet and muddy clothing, stiffening muscles, alternate heat and cold, trifles like these no longer worried them.

There were still some difficult and slippery stretches to be negotiated, where the rocks were covered with sticky clay. Then suddenly something new took hold of their attention, at first unconsciously, then more impellingly, finally becoming an obsession. A noise . . . something muffled, diffused, which irritated their eardrums, going on and on, seeming to come from nowhere and yet from everywhere at once. At least it seemed so in the beginning.

After a while it could be given a name: it was a roar, the kind of roar which would come from a large waterfall. Suddenly the noise drowned everything. Just beside them the stream rolled down into space, and the thunder of its fall, amplified by the roof and the walls, held them motionless at the entrance of yet another cave.

"It's crazy," said Théodor, who was more stirred than ever before, "but I've an idea that we have come right through the mountain and out into the night outside."

He turned towards Lépineux.

"Tell me, Georges. What time is it?"

Lépineux merely shrugged his shoulders. It was a childish idea; but he took a quick glance at his wrist-watch all the same. It was half-past six in the evening. "It's August and still broad daylight," he said ironically.

The three men were now well and truly at the bottom of the pot-hole, and they lit a new flare. In the sudden burst of light which followed they saw a cave so long that its lower part lay plunged in darkness. Lépineux, Théodor and Epelly all agreed that they were nearer the roof than the floor. Their gallery had, in fact, opened out on to the top of a cliff, the foot of which was invisible. It was difficult to guess its height; it might be a hundred and fifty feet, three hundred or perhaps four fifty.

"We shall know soon enough," bellowed Epelly, through the roar of the waterfall, as he started to make fast a rope for their return trip later.

He went down without too much difficulty, but when he let go of the rope some hundred and fifty feet farther down, he saw that he was on top of yet another cliff.

"It's a cave within a cave," he muttered.

It was, in fact, a vast slope of loose fallen rocks which he had now to tackle without falling. He shouted to tell the other two on top to come down, but neither Lépineux nor Théodor budged.

"How can we tell what it is he wants!" growled the Belgian. "Does he want us to hoist him up again because he is in trouble on the ledge, or does he want us to go down after him?"

So Epelly had to clamber all the way back up the cliff to tell them that the way was clear. This time they all went down in complete darkness.

They had lost count of how many hours they had been in getting to this vast pebbly beach where they were now standing, but obviously they had reached the bottom at last, the very bottom of this hall of Titans, and to walk on level ground was almost a rest. They walked on about thirty yards, following the river, now flowing peacefully, and crossed some sandbeds before meeting rocks again a little farther on.

Suddenly Lépineux seized the arm of the man nearest to him. The river had disappeared into the ground and a huge wall of dark black limestone rose up in front of them, barring their way. It was three hundred feet high, and a cathedral tower would have seemed small beside it.

"I think," Lépineux said quietly, "I think this time we shall get no farther. We really have reached bottom."

THE SURVEYORS AT WORK

"I wake up very uncomfortable and wet through. Everything is wet everywhere. My back aches with cold. I reach out an arm. Horrors! It's four times wetter outside. I look at the time. Nine o'clock. Yes, but is it evening or morning? Think! If it's evening, I have slept twenty-four hours. That's clearly too much. Then it must be nine in the morning. Time to get up."

So wrote Michel Letrône in his notebook on the morning of some forgotten day, fifteen or sixteen hundred feet underground at the opening to an unexplored cave. He was forbidden to give it a name, because that agreeable task belonged to the team on the spot. He had had no news of them for twenty-four hours, though presumably they were going on into the unknown down there, five hundred or a thousand yards farther on, perhaps more; and perhaps even fifteen hundred or three thousand feet farther down.

Jo Ballandreaux was busy at his side . . . again the pen ran across the page of Letrône's little notebook . . .

"Jo, opening an eye, saw me irresolute and said pitilessly: 'It's nine o'clock. Time to get up. There's work to do.'

" 'That beastly word again! Why must you talk about work at this hour of the morning. What a brute you are!'

" 'Too bad, old man, but we've got to get on!'

" 'All right. I'll get up.'

" I pulled on my underclothes, which I had been trying to dry in my sleeping bag; then my overalls, which were still wet. After a night under canvas there's no more disagreeable sensation I know of. I thrust my feet out and pushed them quickly into my boots, laced on my leggings, took my belt and my helmet.

" Jo was already outside. He was cleaning and refilling his acetylene lamp.

" 'You must do yours, too,' he said, and held out his own tin of carbide. 'We'll keep yours for the bottom,' he added maliciously.

" Turning to heat the coffee, I was furious to find the stove we had brought with us was empty. I threw the blame on Jo, who was in no way responsible, but he took it in good part. So there we were, condemned to go without hot food for two days. To think that we had brought the stove this far! Breakfast on tinned milk and tinned meat, both cold, and that was all. We hadn't much food and would have to go carefully.

" By ten o'clock we were all ready, with rubber mattresses and sleeping bags all rolled and packs done up. Then we took the road into the unknown. Where were we bound? We knew nothing, and we could only guess the end of it. A flooded shaft, a *siphon*, an obstruction, what would it produce?

" The same old game went on all the time: climb, stop, take sights; notebook, pencil, compass. Over and over again, acrobatics, stop, take sights; notebook, pencil, compass."

The rendezvous with the forward party took place about noon on the second day. Hampered by their measuring instruments, and working slowly from sight to sight, Letrône and Ballandreaux gradually approached the waterfall, while Lépineux, Epelly and Théodor, after examining the great wall from below and appraising the really astonishing size

Top left: Quéffelec with the switchboard which he designed for the winch used in 1953 and 1954 (*below*). *Top right*: the auto-lift used by Bidegain in the last stages of the ascent.

ANDRE MAIREY

ROBERT J. LEVI

of this latest cave (now named " La Verna ") had packed up
and were retracing their steps.

Lépineux, who was in the lead on the climb up, reached
the top of the cliff just as Ballandreaux had finished setting
up his theodolite there.

It was a great moment. In honour of the meeting, the
flask of rum which was reserved for special occasions
appeared again and they all took a good swig. Epelly no
doubt went at it more whole-heartedly than the others, for,
the time having come for the surveyors to make the descent,
he went up to Letrône and, with some feeling, shouted in
his ear:

" Michel, tell us that we are the lowest creatures in the
world. Give us a thumping big figure!"

No one burst out laughing, probably because everyone
deep down in his heart was ready to echo his anguished cry.
But they had to be patient for a few hours longer. Letrône
and Ballandreaux went down slowly, stopped frequently,
took notes and made additions. At long last, when they had
reached the final barrier and had written all their figures
down, excitement had reached fever pitch.

" How deep?" asked Lépineux in a whisper.

And Letrône answered:

" 2,152 feet. Yes, exactly that. 2,152 feet!"

The door of hope closed with a bang. They looked at one
another in silence and the noise of the waterfall seemed
suddenly louder.

ON THE SURFACE

On 15 August, at three o'clock in the afternoon, the telephone from the bottom rang at last.

" Hullo?"

Casteret had rushed to the receiver; we saw his face grow
thoughtful and then after a while brighten suddenly, and he
turned to those standing round and said:

" It's Lépineux! "

For three days we had been without news of B party. Before leaving the base camp it had disconnected the telephone at the bottom of the shaft and remained without any contact at all with the surface while it went on into the unknown. An accident could have happened to one of the party without our knowing anything of it until long afterwards.

On leaving the hole with A party, Casteret had wasted no time in going, with Dr Mairey, to see Loubens's parents. He explained to them as kindly as he could that it would be impossible to bring the body up that year. The camp, when he left it, was happy and comparatively calm, but he returned to find it excited and on edge. In thought we were all with Lépineux, not only the members of the expedition, but the shepherds too, the reporters, the onlookers, the French gendarmes and the Spanish carabineers. So when Casteret said " It's Lépineux " the reaction was immediate. The whole camp rushed to the telephone. A fever seized us as it had seized the men underground, but then it was the fever of discovery; this time it was a fever of anxiety to know what was happening. To know at once and to be the first to know, before the others. We could hear Casteret saying:

" Four caves? Did you say you have discovered four more caves? That's wonderful! "

There was a short silence and then Casteret's face darkened slightly; very slightly, but it was obvious to those around him. Several times he repeated: " How much? How much?" And this question was followed by an " Ah!" without enthusiasm. We did not know what to think.

The mystery was only cleared up when the conversation ended.

" Well, there it is," he said quite simply. " Party A has reached the bottom of the chasm, and the last cave is 2,152 feet deep."

" But it's tremendous," someone said.

" Of course it is," Casteret admitted. " And a little exasperating too. The world's deepest cave, the Trou du Glaz, is

2,158 feet deep, and Pierre Saint-Martin misses the record by barely six feet."

All the same our explorations had gone well and the discovery of such important caves made the expedition a complete success. When someone spoke slightingly of what had been achieved Casteret replied:

"That's absurd, my boy. Records mean very little. We are not here to set up records, but to strengthen our characters, and refine them by making contact with a side of Nature that is little known to us; and develop the spirit of comradeship, and perhaps in time be of assistance to science and the national economy. Above all, we are here for the joy of exploring a cave with no preconceived object in view."

To Casteret the joy of underground exploration was no empty phrase, and once it was decided that a third party, to be called C party, was to be formed, composed of himself, Mairey and Lévi, a party which would in a way set an official seal on the achievement of B party, he could hardly wait to be on the move; and his impatience made him the hero of the mule story.

Casteret was sitting at the edge of the shaft beside the winch, when a Basque porter came along to tell him that a mule-train, which they had been waiting for impatiently, was at last in sight and would soon reach the camp. Seizing the telephone which connected the entrance to the shaft with the camp higher up the mountain side, he called out:

"Hullo there! The mules are arriving. Get them unloaded as soon as they reach you and bring over the new parachute harnesses they've sent us from Pau."

A voice replied:

"What mules? We aren't expecting any mules."

"But of course we are! They're the mules that left Arette village this morning. Can't you see them? I'm told they're in sight."

"Can we see the mules?" answered the voice. "No, we can't. And we should be surprised to see them reach here. Very surprised indeed. And we should certainly like to see them!"

"Come on, now," said Casteret. "This is absurd. Are you all blockheads? Hullo, there! Who's at the telephone?"

This last remark was greeted with a loud shout of laughter and then Casteret heard the voice say:

"Here? It's Lépineux!"

B party's leader was still underground, at the bottom of the approach shaft. Casteret had merely picked up the wrong telephone, the two instruments being side by side, and had tried to convince Lépineux that he was about to witness the arrival of the mule-train—twelve hundred feet underground!

The whole camp roared with laughter, and the disappointment over the depth which Lépineux's party had reached was almost forgotten; everyone laughed and went on working as usual, just as if nothing sensational had been happening or had nearly happened.

Then, just as Casteret was getting ready to go down the shaft, some humorist with an anxious look on his face walked up to him and asked:

"Aren't you going to take a pick down with you?"

"A pick?" asked Casteret with astonishment. "No, whatever for?"

"Why, to make the hole deeper, of course! It wouldn't take long to dig six more feet!"

And Casteret vanished into the shaft amid a final peal of laughter.

TRUTH AT THE BOTTOM OF THE WELL

Down in the string of caves which make up the Pierre Saint-Martin hole, Casteret, Lévi and Mairey were busy with a fourth member of their party, dumb but valuable, an altimeter. It belonged to Casteret, who had taken the greatest care of it all through the expedition, keeping it swaddled up like a small child and forbidding anyone to touch it. The airmen at the Pau base had entrusted it to him, with strict instructions that he was to return it to them, when he had finished with it, just as he had received it. He unveiled it at last at the foot of the Great Barrier, and it was quite a ceremony. Then, after a rest, the three men went on, following the fluorescent marks left by their predecessors.

B party had done its work under the impulse of pure discovery, but C party, with an expert spelaeologist, a doctor and a trained administrator, tried to make a step-by-step analysis and a thorough examination of the ground covered, amounting, in fact, to the second stage of exploration.

Casteret has himself described it very well: " The crossing of the Adélie cave, like that of all the caves in the hole, took the form of an endless series of wild acrobatics across a scene of mythological chaos. In their war against the gods, the giants piled Pelion on Ossa in order to climb Olympus. Could it have been a similar war of Titans that took place here? No, here the giants are called Tectonics, Erosion and Fissuration; it was to natural agents, to hydrogeological phenomena, that we owed this architecture so utterly beyond man's compass: naves of such height and so prodigious in their size, and the chaos of huge boulders that had fallen from their roofs.

" These piles of boulders, reaching a hundred or a hundred and fifty feet high, blocked the floor of the caves; they grew larger and larger, and were always being reformed and reshaped by the fury and measureless force of the water, which undermined, dismembered and carried away everything in its path.

" Though caves usually impart an impression of calm, immobility and thousand-year-old serenity, it was quite different here. This was a cave in mid-evolution, a young cave—geologically speaking—a living cave where the forces of Nature were actively at work and in battle. Clearly visible on the walls and the roof were the fresh scars where tons of rock had broken loose or crumbled away and been hurled down to the cave floor below.

" The floor of primeval rock was nowhere to be seen, being completely covered by the enormous boulders over

which you had to move with the greatest care and circum-
spection, for everything was liable to shift. Some boulders,
as large as houses, bore traces of collapse which proved that
they were 'working.' Others, not so big, were trembling, as
it were, and unstable; and you had to be ready to let go
abruptly of any piece of rock you had taken hold of, because
it at once started to move towards you. You might have to
shift your foothold hurriedly or even jump, because the
boulder you were walking on started to tremble under you.
All around, you could see numberless new star-shaped impressions made by projectiles of all sizes, which had fallen
from the roof above.

"All this gave the Pierre Saint-Martin hole a peculiar
feeling of insecurity and hostility, a constant atmosphere of
danger and fear, from which no one, believe me, could
escape. Everything was dominated by an obsession with the
ever-present possibility of a serious accident, followed by
rescue operations, the difficulty of which it was unnecessary
to exaggerate."

All the same, the three men reached a cairn built by B
party with no bones broken and no sprains. As Lévi bent
down, the light from the lamp on his forehead played over
the pile of stones, and in the glare of it he read the words
"Topographer's Camp.—G. B. M. L."

Casteret, Lévi and Mairey were now on the spot where
Ballandreaux and Letrône had passed their first night in
unexplored territory, right in the middle of the cave later
known as the Salle Adélie. Steadily and without hurrying,
C party pursued its way, encountering the same difficulties
which had compelled the others to exercise all their skill and
ingenuity. They also found the small ledge beside the water
where they had to remove their packs before passing along
it. Casteret took advantage of this pause to take a glance at
the altimeter.

"Seventeen hundred feet," he grumbled. "We still have
to go down another 450 feet."

They reached the La Verna cave after nine hours walking,
crawling and sliding. Coming out at the famous wall of rock

where the torrent made its rush before leaping into space, they felt the same impression of terror mingled with respect and admiration that Théodor, Epelly and Lépineux had already experienced. The same road, the same reaction . . . in fact they were only repeating what the others had already accomplished.

And yet, no! For at the bottom of the hole, at the point where it ends and the river is swallowed up, at the foot of the final wall itself, they had an amazing shock.

Casteret unwrapped his altimeter once again. Its glass was cracked, but the needle was still intact; he placed the instrument carefully on the ground.

" No," said Lévi, jokingly pointing a finger to a hollow at the foot of the wall. " Try over there. That will give us three more feet!"

But Casteret had stopped laughing. Utter stupefaction was written on his face. As his acetylene lamp shone on the dial, he could not take his eyes from the figure he was reading.

" Lévi! Mairey! Come and look for yourselves. I wonder if my sight is failing!"

The two men bent down in turn, and their faces took on expressions of unutterable astonishment.

" But then . . ." stammered the doctor, " they were mistaken! Quite mistaken! The hole is not 2,152 feet deep. If this instrument is right, and why shouldn't it be, this hole is not 2,152 feet deep."

AN UNEXPECTED TELEPHONE CALL

On 18 August, at nine in the morning, Bidegain was working near the entrance to the hole when he was called to the telephone. He raised the receiver calmly enough, knowing that it could only be Casteret and his two companions.

" Well, is everything O.K.?" he asked. " No new discoveries in the lateral galleries?"

" Galleries!" exclaimed Casteret down below. " There are

no lateral galleries. None. That was all an illusion, quite excusable in its way, caused by the vast size of the caves."

Bidegain pulled a long face. By and large this Pierre Saint-Martin hole had brought nothing but disappointment; Loubens had died for nothing.

He bent over the receiver:

" So, there's nothing for you to do but come up?"

" Exactly!"

Then Casteret added:

" There's one thing more! The topographers are wrong in their calculations. The hole is not 2,152 feet deep."

Bidegain's face grew still longer.

" That's fine," he exclaimed, and there was bitterness breaking into his voice. " It will soon turn out to be a little hole made of nothing."

But Casteret went on:

" Just a minute! Don't let's exaggerate. It won't interest you, of course, to know the exact depth of the Pierre Saint-Martin hole, will it?"

" Oh! Get on with it. Let's hear the whole story."

" It's 2,394 feet deep! Letrône and Ballandreaux must have forgotten to add in several angles. We are in the deepest cave in the world!"

There was no reply. Bidegain had dropped the telephone, and we saw him wave his arms like a madman and we knew at once that something out of the ordinary had happened. His face shone; he was jubilant, but incapable of putting two intelligible phrases together. At last, we heard him say:

" We've done it! We've done it, boys! It's 2,394 feet!"

There was a rush. Ballandreaux and Letrône had to fetch their notebook and they started to go over their calculations again, and Quéffelec went over the figures with them. In time they found their mistake; something had been left out; all the figures had not been added in.

" Casteret . . . Casteret! Are you still there?" And as Casteret could only answer with an amused " Yes," Bidegain shouted:

"The Lyons boys have rechecked their figures, and they now make it 2,388 feet."

"Well, that's fine! I am all for strict scientific accuracy and so the last figure—the smaller one—becomes the official figure."

On the bare mountain top, where the *doline* opened, someone was playing an accordion and the tune rose gaily to the sky above.

The team had not worked for nothing; and Loubens had not died in vain.

Chapter Four

WHAT IS THE USE?

N

o one in C party said anything momentous when they reached the bottom of the hole and, after correcting B party's error in calculation, found that the lowest part of the last cave was 2,394 feet. Casteret was cool as always; he quietly put the altimeter back in his pack and then looked around him with the true spelaeologist's eye, the eye of experience.

This impassivity born of wisdom was at once rewarded. A millipede, colourless and white as snow, was crawling slowly across the side of a boulder. Casteret saw it.

" Mairey," he exclaimed, " here's a myriapod!"

To call the doctor to verify this astonishing discovery was quite natural, as Mairey also bore the official title of entomologist to the expedition. Bending down he caught the little creature and slipped it deftly into a test-tube of alcohol.

" And now," he said, " we possess the world's lowest insect."

Mairey had spoken without any humorous intention at all; Casteret, too, listened without a smile, and Lévi, who was watching them both, had suddenly the clearest possible impression that the existence of this tiny creature at a depth of two thousand four hundred feet in a cave that had neither vegetation nor light moved them more than their own presence underground or the fact of their being the holders of a coveted record.

People have said, " What is the use of going down holes?" The reaction of these two spelaeologists is one answer, for,

by its results, spelaeology has been shown to be more than
a game. It sets itself precise scientific objects; it is of importance to others as well as to those who go down the shafts
and cross the giant galleries. What has never been mentioned in the newspapers, because it is sensational only in
the eyes of specialists, is that the Pierre Saint-Martin
explorers have collected among the boulders in the caves
eight different amphibious creatures living a retarded
existence, the descendants of species that disappeared
millions of years ago, but which in bygone times used to
be found on the earth's surface; fossils not yet dead, like
the famous cœlacanth fish, the study of which furnished
valuable information about the shape of continents and seas
in geological epochs long past.

Ask Dr Jeannel, of the Museum, what he thinks of the
stupid, cynical question, "What is the use?" Among the
discoveries at Pierre Saint-Martin were two specimens
belonging to a new species. Nothing much, perhaps, but it
can be argued that it is by means of tiny clues like these that
science progresses, however slowly. The scientists have
followed the example of the spelaeologists who named one
of the caves in the pot-hole after their companion who died
there, and have aptly used the same name to classify the new
species. Since 1953 a new species of insects has existed
known as *Aphaenops Loubensi.*

Never before has man been so eager to explore the
unknown, and never before, perhaps, has man been so ready
to criticise this eagerness. Too many people still imagine
that a scientist is someone who works within four walls,
studying life from books and keeping strictly to the laboratory. Nothing, in fact, is farther from the truth. Science is
an adventure, and every adventure involves taking risks.
The crew of the Kon-Tiki, Bombard, the men who explored
the Orinoco and the Amazon, and the divers who searched
for deep-sea treasure, all faced risks; and before them there
had been Schliemann and the Egyptologists.

One aspect of the Pierre Saint-Martin explorations has
never been disclosed in the newspapers, the hundreds of

facts and observations, geological and mineralogical, relating
to erosion, temperature, air currents, mist condensation and
ionisation, which Casteret and his companions collected.

The Pierre Saint-Martin explorers were not content to go
up and down the pot-hole in the same way as people take a
ride on a scenic railway at a country fair, just for the thrill
of it.

It was in 1951 that Loubens discovered the underground
river, and in the years that followed, experiments were
carried out by putting fluorescein into the water, and it was
found that the river emerged into the open three miles farther
on in the valley of Sainte-Engrâce. All that will now be
needed is a tunnel several hundred yards long connecting
the La Verna cave with the mountain side; this will take the
river and divert it into a conduit from which the water will
plunge eighteen hundred feet to the turbines of a hydro-
electric station.

Can anyone still say, " What is the use?" The people of
the Sainte-Engrâce valley have no electricity; they will get
it. The whole region is short of water; it will get it. France
always needs more electric power, and she will get several
million more kilowatts.

But even supposing that there had been no water in Pierre
Saint-Martin, no strange insects at the bottom of the pot-
hole, and no valuable studies to be made of the nature of
the subsoil, is there any reason to criticise an enthusiasm for
normal healthy adventure? It is a bad habit of ours to want
everything to serve some practical purpose. By strictly
utilitarian standards, a poem serves no useful end, nor does
a symphony, nor a picture, and yet we would not think of
criticising those who devote their lives to art—and what
would our lives be without art? Adventure is something akin
to a work of art shaped out of life—mankind is the better
for it, and it is encouraging in an age when we are
imprisoned by material interests to see someone spending
his energies on excelling himself, without getting a penny
in return.

The young man who has the courage to risk his life

climbing a mountain, or exploring some dangerous terrain, or crossing an ocean, or going down a pot-hole, will never turn out to be mean-spirited, never become an outsider or a social misfit. He has proved himself in meeting the challenge of that kind of adventure which offers no material rewards, and he will prove himself again in the adventure where there are many rewards to be won, the adventure we call life.

The exploration of the Pierre Saint-Martin pot-hole has taught us above all an effective lesson in moral values.

THIS PRECIOUS THREAD

Some people, whose idea of high adventure is a well-organised motor coach tour, are simple enough to believe that an expedition like that to Pierre Saint-Martin can be undertaken in the vacation by a few students picked at random, and that given both the opportunity and the desire, down the shaft you go on the end of a length of cable, attached to some machine or other. They would be very surprised to be told that they were rather wide of the mark and that the exploration of an important pot-hole can only be successful if backed by sound organisation.

In the Pierre Saint-Martin expedition every member had his own job to do. The man on the winch did not go down the shaft and the man below ground did not take charge of surface operations. We have already seen how the exploration of the unknown that lay between the 1,200 and the 2,400 feet levels was not left to chance; one party being detailed for reconnaissance, another for marking the route to be followed and for ensuring that it was clearly marked, and a third for making the necessary topographical surveys. Discipline is the first essential in a good spelaeologist. Imagine the reaction of the men down below if, for example, they had found that the winch was sometimes left unattended. They would have lost confidence—and failure would have been inevitable.

Marcel Loubens's death, being the direct consequence of

a mechanical defect, was a severe setback which had to be overcome. That had happened in 1952, and if the 1953 expedition was to be a success, all concerned had to have complete faith in the winch, and this could only be restored when concrete proofs had been given of its efficiency. When Quéffelec, who was the expert on these things, arrived with his winch at Pierre Saint-Martin, he brought with him what was obviously a different machine, but one which had already seen service. His object was to reassure the team; this particular winch had been tested frequently, in fact, throughout the previous year and the results had been carefully checked.

There were always several men round the winch at the top of the shaft, Janssens, Pierre Louis, Naudin and others too; one of them to work it, another to take charge of the ascent and descent of anyone working in the shaft and to keep in touch with him over the microphone, a third to help the explorers in and out of their clothes, and a fourth to look after the petrol supply. This went on night and day. The surface party was divided into two shifts, the first working from daybreak until three o'clock in the afternoon, and the second from six in the evening until two next morning. Work generally stopped during the hottest part of the afternoon and in the small hours of the night. It was all rather like the civil servant's daily grind, and a mighty responsible one, too.

Without these men who worked in the shade of the side-lines (metaphorical shade, of course, because it can be horribly hot up there), the team who formed the spearhead of the expedition could never have succeeded. In naming one of the vast Pierre Saint-Martin caves the Quéffelec cave (the fourth, immediately after the Métro), Lépineux paid a well-deserved tribute to this engineer, who had not been afraid to assume the heavy burden of responsibility for supplying a new winch. As they watched the power winch working for the first time, their thoughts must have gone back to Max Cosyns's pedal winch, whose failure—people have talked of negligence—led to the Loubens disaster.

Quéffelec's winch arrived in sections and soon became the

star turn at Pierre Saint-Martin. It was all-electric, the current being supplied by a three-kilowatt generating set. It weighed over nine hundred pounds and was fitted with a non-gyratory cable three hundred and eighty yards long, a third of an inch in diameter and weighing two hundred pounds. The spelaeologist was attached to it by a parachute harness, or rather the harness was fixed to a steel cross-bar which was fastened in its turn by two snap-hooks and thimbles to the eye of the cable itself. Each time it was used one of the men on the winch examined the end of the cable which was held firmly in place by two violin-shaped double clamps.

To give added protection, the end of the cable and the clamps were covered by a steel cap, with the express object of preventing it from catching up in a fissure when being sent down the shaft by itself. There was also a cylinder fixed to the base of the cap, looking very much like a shell-case, and so the name clung to it. This protected the microphone and earphones while the cable was being lowered or brought up on its own.

I explained all this to myself a thousand times, though, in fact, I only went down once, after a good many others had done so and in the best possible conditions. But man is so made that he is always a little afraid to entrust his life to a mere machine.

"Look," said Naudin, trying to reassure me, "the electric motor brakes automatically when you stop. It runs at fourteen hundred revolutions a minute and is geared to two multi-grooved pulleys. It's a wonderful device, you know, and even if you weighed a ton you could hitch yourself to the cable and be perfectly safe with pulleys like those!"

"These pulleys," he went on to explain, "are what drives the winch. There's no chance that the cable will slip either when you are moving or when you are stopped, and so you are completely safe. And to make doubly sure, there are more pulleys. Their function is to guide the cable into its proper channels, so to speak, on this drum here, which is driven by the two multi-grooved pulleys. The pull of the drum on the cable is quite small, only enough for winding and unwinding; and so we avoid the risk of it jamming, which happens when the pull of the drum is too strong."

"That's fine," I replied, "but what happens when the winch is in action, and there is someone on the end of the cable?"

"Nothing much," Naudin said, "or let's put it this way. The return-pulley controls a dynamometer which shows on a dial on the switchboard whether everything is normal. If so, there's a green light, and if there's something wrong there's a red light and an alarm bell rings. That happens when the load is too heavy, that's to say when the cable jams and the motor goes on running. As for the load, you can reckon that at a ton or more."

There was no doubt about it, the switchboard was a really fine job. It had a voltmeter, an ammeter, a three-position switch, one for going up, one for stop and one for going down, fuse boxes, a chronometer for timing an operation, and a plug for the winch lighting, which Quéffelec used for his electric razor. Depth was shown by the chronometer, or on a dial marked in metres and controlled by the cable-drum. In fact, the winch had everything.

I asked one last question.

"Suppose the cable—broke, what weight would there have to be on it? I mean, what's the maximum load?"

Naudin laughed. "Father," he said, "you will have to weigh well over two tons before we refuse to lower you, so there's a good margin of safety, but when the load reaches the ton mark, we go pretty carefully, I can tell you."

I had to leave him then, as it was time for me to prepare supper—being, if you remember, the expedition's cook-boy that year.

AROUND AND ABOUT THE POT-HOLE

As the poisoning of my fellow-men is not at all to my taste, my days were not confined to cooking, and I, too, did a

MAX COSYNS

JACQUES LABEYRIE

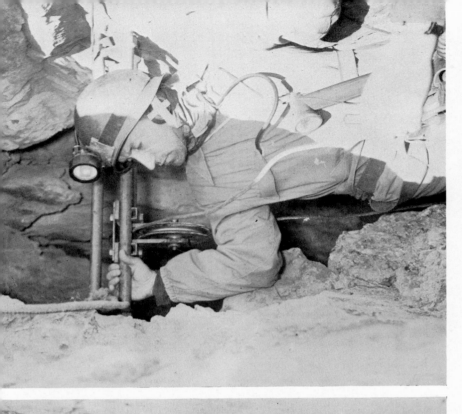

little pot-holing with several of my friends. The country round us was a complete Gruyère cheese, with one really important hole, the Pierre Saint-Martin, or Lépineux cave, and a multitude of ordinary small holes. But ordinary though they were, they were none the less interesting and experienced members of the team were not above going down them if only to keep in practice.

I went down the " Trou du Vent " with the Lyons scouts, who rather specialised in these minor holes. They had one thought in mind—to find another way down into the depths underground, and they paid pleasant little visits to shafts dotted all over the mountain side. It was, of course, the five Lyons scouts who were missing from the Franco-Spanish lunch party given in the big tent on the day the explorations began. They were busy swimming and diving in frogmen's kit somewhere in the Sainte-Engrâce valley, some four thousand feet down the mountain side. They knew that the underground river appeared somewhere there, and were looking for the spot where it emerged, or a way down to it.

The " Trou du Vent " is a pleasant little hole discovered by the shepherds, and so called because there is a moist breeze coming from it and if you hold a piece of paper by the opening it will be blown away. The Lyons scouts and I explored it for the very simple reason that we felt an interest in it. In 1953 we were only just beginning to explore Pierre Saint-Martin and only a third of its secrets had been revealed, the Lépineux, Casteret and Loubens caves—the others were not discovered until a few days later. The " Trou du Vent " lay above the presumed course of the underground river and we had the idea that it might lead down to it, perhaps because the thermometer reading at the opening to the shaft was forty degrees, exactly the temperature at the bottom of the Lépineux and adjoining caves.

" Just think," whispered Ballandreaux in my ear, " we make a nice descent with our rope ladders, and drop right on top of Casteret, with his cable, winch and all the paraphernalia that goes with it. That would be a joke, wouldn't it?"

MPSM 7

We set off on 8 August at ten o'clock in the morning; no reporters and no publicity. The atmosphere was every bit the same as that of Pierre Saint-Martin, but the Press were not interested. A thick mist lay all around us and cut visibility down to ten yards, and it took us an hour and a half to find the entry to the shaft. It was no use running about up there like madmen; the loads we carried made this impossible and any false move could pitch us down into the bowels of the earth, as the country consisted of a great many holes with a little solid ground around them.

We put our gear on quickly—two pullovers, paratrooper's overalls, helmet, lamp, hammer, *pitons,* rope ladders, nothing was forgotten. By then it was noon, and we drew lots for the order in which we should go down. Jo Ballandreaux was was first, then Michel Letrône, myself, Epelly and Théodor. Milou Ballandreaux and Ruiz, the Spaniard, took charge of the surface end of the rope.

I cast off with a sixty-foot length of ladder and the great adventure began. After all, no one had been down this pothole before, and it might well prove just as formidable as the other big one. Had it not been for the crows that had been frightened by Lépineux's stone, perhaps no one would ever have thought of exploring Pierre Saint-Martin. I had time to think about that while I waited on a small ledge of rock a hundred feet down. The expedition was going ahead as expected, that is, slowly. Ballandreaux and Letrône had fastened their rope ladders securely with their *pitons* and became the connecting link with the rest of us. They reached 150 feet, but before that they had spent a good half-hour cleaning up " my " ledge. There was music in the shaft, real modern music, the music of stones falling and rolling on and on. Instinctively I put my hand to my head to make sure my helmet was still keeping it properly covered.

The first feeling we had of real exploring was when we were all three together on the 150 foot ledge. It was more than a ledge, and was really a small room, or ante-chamber to the unknown. At the end was a gallery which narrowed away out of sight. Where could it lead?

We examined it and had to admit, reluctantly, that it lead nowhere, except to a shaft which rose parallel to our own, but had no outlet. Nothing more than a decoy, in fact. And so the descent went on, amid the monotonous surroundings of friable grey rock and without any stalagmites or stalactites to give it character. I was tempted to write it off, but I didn't quite dare to yet— there might be a happy surprise waiting for us down below.

At two hundred feet down we knew how deep the shaft was. We landed on a comfortable ledge, not too sloping and with room to move. We cleared it in twenty minutes and lowered a plummet to find out what awaited us lower down. It was impressive, all right—a sheer drop of two hundred and fifty feet.

" Two-fifty—two-fifty," grumbled Letrône. " I should say three hundred. Is somebody going to tell *them*?"

" Them " was a disdainful reference to Théodor and Epelly farther up the shaft. We had none of the wonderful equipment which was available at Pierre Saint-Martin— telephone, microphone, loudspeaker—and we had to manage with a device which never breaks down, the human voice. We shouted as loud as we could, carefully separating each syllable, and asked " them " to send down another three hundred feet of rope ladder and some proper spelaeologist's equipment, thermometer, paper, pencil and candles for surveying.

A good half-hour later, Théodor and Epelly had both joined us, the first taking twenty minutes and the other fifteen. Epelly at once assumed an air of competence and took first place on the rope.

" I will lead," he explained, " and Jo and Michel will follow and make the survey. You, Jimmy, and you, Father, can stay here to see us safely down. You will only follow if it proves worth while."

It was now half past three and we all agreed to eat the food we had brought with us before going on. Then, throwing three hundred feet of rope ladder into space, Epelly began to descend. It was a long and dangerous business. We

MPSM 7*

heard the sinister sound of stones whistling down the shaft
and falling with a shattering noise below him. Then all was
silent. We looked at one another in dismay. Had something
happened to Epelly?

"Dan. . . . Hullo, Dan. . . ."

We heaved a sigh of relief when we heard him say :

"Well, what is it?"

Epelly's voice reached us, calm and very much alive. He
showed no signs of uneasiness and was quite obviously
resting a moment to survey his progress.

Time went on and once again we heard the music of the
stones, nerve-racking and monotonous. At first we could
still hear Dan's heavy breathing, but now he was so far off
that no sign of his presence in the shaft reached us, and soon
even the sound of stones knocking against one another became muffled, and in time barely audible. Only the steady
paying off of the safety rope at our feet reassured us, and at
last that too ceased to move.

"He must have reached the bottom," Théodor murmured.

We kept ourselves amused as best we could during the
long wait on the ledge, whistling a scrap of a tune, or letting
memories flood back. Casteret's phrase, "patience and
imagination," was often in our minds and we kept thinking
of Milou and Ruiz up top.

Suddenly Théodor grasped my arm.

"Listen!"

I strained my ears. A cavernous voice rose from the
depths. It was Epelly. What was he saying? But I understood
all too soon.

"Fin . . . ish . . . ed! It's . . . all . . . choked . . . up!"

I looked at Théodor in dismay. He shrugged his shoulders;
our dream had vanished. There was to be no joining up with
the Pierre Saint-Martin hole this way, and no taking the
rise out of the others.

When Epelly rejoined us, he told us what had happened.
"You land on a small heap of fallen rocks," he said. "There
is a cave opening up at the foot of it with a lake in the
middle, but it is very, very small. On the right I thought I

could see something which might have been a *siphon*, but it was quite impassable, which means there's no outlet."

" And the depth of *our* hole?" Théodor asked.

I felt he would have liked to have said your hole, but he is a good-natured lad.

" 490 feet at most." We made wry faces. Not even half " their " shaft.

* * * * *

Night was falling when we reached the surface. Two shep-herds had come to join us and they helped us to pack up our equipment. Before leaving, we carefully covered over the " Trou du Vent," in case some wretched sheep should go and end its days in it. And so we got back to the camp at last, near the *doline* where great things were happening and making headlines in the newspapers of all the Western countries. We had forgotten it for a moment, but the real Pierre Saint-Martin was with us again, the hole of holes which admitted no rival.

We had understood.

Chapter Five

1952

LOUBENS'S FALL

W E had understood. The point was that since 16 August 1952 what was a very interesting pot-hole, but only one among many other very interesting pot-holes, had become *the* great hole, the hole that would always spring to mind whenever spelaeology was discussed. It was on 16 August 1952 that Marcel Loubens breathed his last upon a bed of giant stones, after thirty-six hours in the throes of death; and from that moment the whole of France, and all Europe, in fact, began to take a keen interest in spelaeology, a subject which until then the public had ignored, and in this mountain which was unknown to tourists before and only used by the Basque shepherds and their strange breed of sheep.[1]

Yet there was nothing to foretell tragedy. Each August for the past six years parties had gone up to Pierre Saint-Martin and as interest grew equipment improved and organisation took better shape. In 1951 the winch was a kind of bicycle and to work this man-driven machine was the equivalent of cycling ninety miles a day.

In 1952 it was replaced by an electric winch weighing two hundred and twenty pounds, designed by Max Cosyns, an engineer who had accompanied Picard in his ascents into the stratosphere and in his explorations under the sea.

[1] For this and the following chapter, I have relied on Tazieff's account; he was the only eyewitness of the tragedy and he has given a moving description of it in his fine book, *Le Gouffre de la Pierre Saint-Martin* (ed Arthaud).

Everyone felt confident, and so when people asked, " Aren't you afraid to be dangling in a hole nearly twelve hundred feet deep on the end of a cable a fraction of an inch thick?" they all replied, " We never give it a thought."

The imagination was at work on other things; it dreamed of what there was to discover, of following an unknown route that perhaps twelve, fifteen, eighteen hundred feet below ground might lead the intrepid explorer to a way out into the open air in the Kakouetta gorge. Descending on the end of a cable became no more than a matter of routine, " taking the lift," as Loubens was to call it before his last trip, in admiration of the improved methods of descending the shaft.

Only Tazieff, who witnessed the accident, admitted : " I had a premonition. . . . It is absurd and all to easy to say it afterwards, but I am telling the truth, I had a premonition. Not during the operation, not even when leaving Licq-Atheray for the mountain, but before that on the road which leads to the little village. If one of the team was to be lost tragically, I even thought, whose death would cause me the least sorrow?" All the same, he added, this macabre little game had no sense in it; it was nothing serious, and " I never gave it another thought, once I was settled with dear old Bouchet. The winch had not yet arrived and I spent my first day in a nearby meadow without a care in the world and with an intense feeling of *joie de vivre*. Labeyrie was with me, and the owner of the hotel had lent us a discus and some javelins, and we had some fun with them."

IT DOES NOT ALWAYS BRING LUCK

They went on with their game, to the amusement of a young village girl who was watching, until interrupted by the sound of an engine. An open car appeared at the turn of the road, stopped dead beside the field and a tall cheerful chap popped up like a jack-in-the-box.

"Hey! Look at the champions!"

Had Tazieff or Labeyrie been in any doubt about who the newcomer was, his accent would have dispelled it. It was Marcel Loubens, and when he said "champions" he rolled the "m"—if you come from Toulouse, why hide the fact? He did not wait for the other two to ask him to join in, but getting out of his car he peeled off his jacket, picked up a discus, which he had no idea at all how to throw, had it explained to him in a few words, and with all the strength of a fine physique, threw it as far as he could. A loud burst of laughter greeted his throw—the discus had landed right in the middle of a pat of cow dung.

"Fine! Fine!" he cried happily. "That's said to be lucky. I'm going to discover something down the hole! You'll see!"

Loubens had been caving since he was seventeen under the instruction of Norbert Casteret, the most experienced of spelaeologists, and so the other two said that he would not need that sort of omen for success.

Dr André Mairey arrived next day, just before Cosyns and Théodor who were bringing the winch from Brussels, where it had been made to Cosyns's own design, Cosyns being the well-known Professor of Engineering at the university there. Then Casteret, Janssens, Treuthard and Pierre Louis burst into the lounge of the hotel where in living memory the spelaeologists of those parts had always foregathered. The only one missing was Occhialini, who had discovered the hole with Lépineux in 1950, but as he had to come from Brazil his late arrival was only to be expected.

"And Lépineux?" asked a reporter who had already arrived. "Isn't he coming this year?"

"That would be difficult," replied Loubens with a smile. "He's probably breaking ice just now." And mopping his brow, for it was blazing hot in the valley, he added, "He's luckier than we are." Lépineux, who was a jeweller by profession in Bagnères-de-Bigorre, was on leave from his business and accompanying Frank Liotard to Adélie Land in the Antarctic.

★   ★   ★   ★   ★

The first important task was to set up the winch. Afterwards, in 1953 and 1954, it was carried up the rough mountain road in sections, but in 1952 that had not been thought
of, and so they had to move a packing-case up the mountain,
weighing two hundred and twenty pounds—not exactly a
bagatelle—and measuring six feet by three. It would have
been too much for a mule, and they had to fall back on an
animal that was rare, at least in that part of the world, a
horse.

Tazieff has described that exhausting climb in detail:
" Loading the mules presented no particular difficulty, but
a good deal of time and patience was lost in fixing the
cumbersome and fragile winch to the horse's back. It only
stayed there in the end precariously balanced and needed
a man on each side of the animal to keep it in place during
the five hours climb. This would not have mattered much
if the route had been easy. Unfortunately it was all too often
nothing but a track and extremely difficult to make out amid
a chaos of white rocks, and the escort to the winch had to
perform some astonishing acrobatics to keep level with the
horse, particularly when it quickened its pace in order to
climb the steeper slopes. Pierre Louis, Treuthard and Lévi
took it in turns on the horse's left, while on the right its
owner, a fair-haired Béarnais with blue eyes, performed
some prodigious feats."

Once the forest was left behind the going improved. The
shepherds appeared on the scene and lent a hand which
everyone appreciated.

Afterwards everyone did what he liked best; Cosyns set
the winch up and allowed no one to touch it; Lévi, then the
expedition's steward, was busy sorting out provisions and
equipment in one of the huts which Lagrâve, the magistrate
turned shepherd, had placed at his disposal; and Mairey
checked his medical supplies. The others were underground
men and having no special jobs up top they had nothing to
do but discuss how long it would take to go down with the
new harness and winch, and ask after the bruises on someone's legs or someone else's cramp. Would there be break-

downs and had they been allowed for? Someone said, " You'll reach the bottom in half an hour, if all goes well, of course. Man proposes. God disposes," he added.

Preparations were complete by the evening of 8 August, and they could hardly have been more vital. By midday on the ninth all was ready for someone to go down the shaft. Lots were drawn and the luck of the draw went to Marcel Loubens, who was best qualified and the most likeable of them all. Of course, there was nothing he wanted more and he reckoned it a stroke of luck to be the first to explore a shaft that had been left for a year. He was in high spirits and dressed quickly, putting on his white crash helmet, collecting his lamps, strapping on his pack, adjusting his earphones and fastening the red throat-microphone round his neck.

ETERNAL NIGHT

" Put up the safety rope," Cosyns ordered.

Casteret got up and began to rope the *doline* off, to prevent the more inquisitive reporters and sightseers getting in the way. Loubens waited at the entry to the shaft ready to slide down into it, and a little later Casteret joined him. Everyone was in good spirits, the weather was fine, there was a blue sky overhead with light fleecy clouds, the winch was working well on the edge of the *doline,* and there was laughter in the air.

" Ready!" cried Loubens. Then with a wave of the hand to Casteret : " *Au revoir, papa,*" he called. He used to look upon himself as Casteret's spiritual son, but this was the first time that he had addressed him so.

Casteret replied in the same playful way, " Goodbye, son." Little did he know that he was really saying goodbye.

It was now up to the men on the winch. Loubens hung by his hands to the jack which was wedged cross-wise and on which the return-pulley was lodged. He took another look at the daylight, and then he let himself slide downwards into the hole.

" Down a little more," he ordered.

Cosyns eased some of the slack.

" Stop," Loubens called again.

He had just reached a tiny platform, ten feet below the entrance, and he stopped there to wait while the heavy kitbags were passed down to him containing a great part of the equipment required for the work underground. It was Théodor and Mairey who carried out this ticklish task.

This done, Loubens called for the last time :

" I'm ready. Goodbye, boys. Lower away."

And he disappeared for good into the shaft. The operation went ahead without hitch. As soon as Loubens reached the bottom of the shaft he telephoned to say that all the stores that had been left down there the year before—boxes of chocolate and coffee, solid fuel, and reels of telephone wire— were still there and in good condition. Natural refrigeration had done its work well.

There was nothing more he could do but await the arrival of Tazieff, the expedition's cameraman and photographer, whose job naturally made him number two. He had been scheduled to arrive by three o'clock at the latest, but there was a hitch—the first—with the winch. The drum jammed in winding the cable up and Tazieff was forced to take his equipment off because with the generous help of the sun he was beginning to melt, and he did not put it on again until nightfall.

He finally started down at ten o'clock, by which time it was raining gently. Six hundred feet down the rain became heavier; it was no longer rain from heaven, but a cascade of water which fell on anyone coming down the shaft with the force of a kitchen tap turned full on. Tazieff had met it the year before, and was not pleased to renew the acquaintance; all he noted was that it flowed with exactly the same rhythm as before. Then, when he had only another three hundred feet to go, the walls of the shaft opened out abruptly and the cable began to turn, sweeping the man who hung at the end of it into a sickening spin.

Tazieff had just passed the vaulted roof of the Lépineux cave when a voice came up to him.

" Shall I light a magnesium flare for you?"

It was Loubens's Toulouse accent. They had arranged that Tazieff should take a photograph from that height, and while he used his Leica, Loubens would see to the lighting. But Tazieff, tired after long hours of waiting, had forgotten to get his camera ready and he showed little enthusiasm. Peering down into the void, he called out:

" No, we'll take a picture on the way up. The effect will be just the same. Don't bother to move."

Cosyns was told by telephone of this change of plan, and then Tazieff went on down again towards the bottom, though more slowly than before. He reached it at one in the morning, tired out, and without more ado he mumbled good night and suggesting that Loubens, who had put the tent up in a position sheltered from possible falls of rock, should follow his example, he stretched himself out in his sleeping bag and promptly fell asleep.

It would be pointless to say that they woke in the morning eleven hundred feet below ground, because they got up in the same darkness as they had fallen asleep, and in the same temperature and the same silence.

" What would you say to a little bird singing?" asked Loubens as he slipped into his damp clothes.

" Why not a cock?" Tazieff replied as he bent over the stove. " A cock to wake you up right in the middle of the night."

A heavy " day " lay before them. They planned to pay another visit to the cave they had discovered the year before, and then go on into the unknown. These two men had taken the same plunge in 1951, and they were now to repeat it. They crossed the Elizabeth Casteret cave quickly and without difficulty. What they now sought was an outlet leading into other caves, so that they could penetrate still farther into the depths of the pot-hole. They decided first of all to follow the stream, which was bound to turn into a raging torrent farther on—probably much farther on—if the dull noise which drummed consistently in their ears was anything to judge by. But the stream was a disappointment. The water disappeared abruptly into a *siphon* so narrow that it was quite impossible to swim through it.

"What about that beach you saw last year, when you came through here alone?" asked Tazieff.

"No sign of it, old chap."

They made a thorough search, making their way over stones which lay at the most unlikely angles, but there was no trace of anywhere less chaotic. Tazieff decided at last that his companion must have been dreaming, or have been the victim of a mirage, which would not have been surprising, considering the state of exhaustion they had reached on that previous occasion.

Their search, however, brought its own reward. Towards seven in the evening when they had decided that it was high time to retrace their steps, to avoid alarming those waiting on the telephone and the others who had, perhaps, already come down to join them at the bottom, they stopped dead before the opening to a shaft.

"Shall we go down?" Loubens asked. "A ladder will do it."

Tazieff did not reply at first. Then he picked up a pebble, and threw it into the hole and listened. The sound of the stone ricochetting against the walls came up to them for a long while.

"It's deep all right," he said. "It's the right way, sure enough." Then he added, "No, Marcel, we can't risk going down there at this hour. God knows when we will get back. Let's leave it to the next trip."

Loubens said nothing. He knew that Tazieff was right. He knew, too, that it would be a rather dreary business getting back to the bottom of the shaft.

The reader may well be surprised at the difficulties encountered by the two explorers and wonder why they hesitated so much when in 1953 and 1954 no one even mentioned these bad stretches, giving the impression that there was no more to it than walking along a road. The answer is simple—where Casteret, Lépineux and Lévi were able to rush on in leaps and bounds, there was nothing, absolutely nothing, in 1952. It was not only a blind advance, there was no indication of the right direction, not a single signpost to make the going easier. That was to be the work of the pioneers, of Loubens, Tazieff and of the others who were now waiting for them at the base camp.

Jacques Labeyrie and Beppo Occhialini received them on their return with something better than open arms—hot coffee that they had just made for the purpose. It helped to revive them, and then followed supper consisting of lentils cooked without fat, not because they were on a diet, but because the fat had been forgotten up top. Loubens and Tazieff then fell fast asleep, while Occhialini indulged in a highly philosophical monologue and Labeyrie whistled a Vivaldi concerto.

Next day they all followed the route which Tazieff and Loubens had marked out the day before. This time they made something more than a reconnaissance, Tazieff carrying his photographic gear and the others dividing between them a hundred and twenty pounds of fluorescein to dye the water of the underground river. If it flowed out into the open they would be able to locate it.

They were working in the Elizabeth Casteret cave, the first after the Lépineux cave, which is really only the prolongation of the bottom of the shaft. While Tazieff and Occhialini were busy with the scientific work, Labeyrie and Loubens set off again in search of a way through.

" We found a *siphon* yesterday," Loubens explained. " We must do better today."

" What about the hole you found yesterday?"

" Perhaps . . ."

Loubens was afraid just then of having seen things too big. He knew how Labeyrie would have scoffed if instead of a shaft which would lead to real progress being made, he was shown some wretched little hole that turned out to be blocked fifty feet down.

Events did not confirm these fears of disappointment; quite the reverse. The hole had a second opening, very much lower, which enabled the two men to proceed without ladders. They had only to make their way over rubble for about a hundred yards before entering a cave whose size was difficult to assess, as they had none of the necessary lighting with them. But they could now hear the roar of the torrent very clearly, and one thing was certain, the *siphon* was behind them and they could go on.

"Well, that'll be tomorrow," Labeyrie decided.

Loubens burst out laughing. "I've heard that old song before. You are quite right, of course. We have found the right way and tomorrow we'll do some real work."

He corrected himself at once. "What I mean is, *you* can do some real work. I'm going back to the top. I'm tired and the shoulder I damaged at Henne-Morte is troubling me again. I'll come back when you have finished exploring this vast cave."

"Vast . . ." Labeyrie repeated gently. "Aren't you exaggerating a little. I have rather got the impression that it is a small cave really, and probably the last one. You are talking through your hat."

Loubens shook his head and he did the same back at the camp when they were all together once more.

"I'm no scientist," he maintained, "and no mathematician like this clever chap Labeyrie, but I can feel the cave behind there. . . . I predict that you are going to find something really stupendous."

Labeyrie was listening attentively. He knew that no one present could rival Loubens's experience of caves, but he remained sceptical all the same, until time proved him wrong and Loubens right; but Loubens was never to know it.

So next morning, before the team left to explore the unknown cave which was later to bear his name, Loubens began to dress for the ascent to the surface.

THE LIGHT THAT FELL TOO SOON

Just as Loubens was getting ready to fasten himself to the cable, someone on the winch telephoned to say there was a slight breakdown and he must be patient for five minutes.

"That's great," grumbled Loubens. "We know their five minutes. As long as they don't make me wait here an hour or two with all this harness on—it's just right for my bad shoulder!"

Labeyrie took advantage of the delay to return to the attack on the subject of the size of the cave. He had been thinking it over and his mathematical turn of mind refused to accept Loubens's intuition.

"What it amounts to," he said suddenly, "is that we've seen nothing positive. Don't go shouting your head off up there about a fantastic pot-hole (he pronounced it *fan-tass-tic*, gently mimicking Loubens's accent). If it doesn't turn out to be so, it's I that will have to report it and I'll be treated like a spoil-sport. I don't make these caves to measure."

But Loubens, with the cable harness on, went on insisting that he *felt* the vast cave. "And I'm convinced," he went on, "that there's much more water still in the parts we have not yet explored. In fact, the show has hardly begun."

"Well, if you are not mistaken, it will be a question of turning it into electricity."

"Suppose," said Tazieff, who had been listening to the argument and now put his oar in, "suppose that the flow was thirty million cubic yards a year, which is quite possible, and that the engineers of the French Electricity Board succeeded in harnessing it, what will they do? Drive a tunnel, a horizontal gallery, coming out on the side of the mountain."

"It's three hundred yards thick," said Labeyrie, who had a liking for precision.

"Thanks. And once this tunnel's made, the water will be sent down a conduit into the valley at Licq."

"No, at Arette," the mathematician countered remorselessly. "We are about four thousand feet up here, and the mountain falls in the direction of Arette which is sixteen hundred feet up."

"All right. What really matters is that it gives a drop of about 2,400 feet. Converted into kilowatts . . ."

Tazieff got no further. Information had just come from the top that the ascent could be made.

"Thank goodness for that," Loubens exclaimed. "I was beginning to stiffen up pretty badly."

Labeyrie still had time to take a photograph, and then to call out : "See that they send us some reinforcements, and make it quite clear that there can never be too many for a tough job like this."

The cable then tightened and Loubens had to climb up a cone-shaped pile of rubble towards the vertical chimney. In his left hand he had a magnesium flare some eighteen inches long, which Tazieff had handed him. He was to light it thirty feet above the bottom, the cameraman's idea being to film someone going up just as he finally disappeared into the vault, the narrow opening of the shaft proper remaining invisible.

When Loubens took off, Tazieff was already in position on the left with a good field of vision.

"What a spin!" cried Loubens.

Round he went, spinning impressively in space for the camera's benefit, and as there was only the light on the front of his helmet to show where he was, he looked strangely like a lighthouse having an attack of giddiness.

"Stop."

Loubens found himself motionless, dangling in space thirty feet up, about the height of a three-storey building. He lit a match, then another, then a third. Tazieff was waiting on his pile of rocks but the indispensable flare refused to light. Marcel's voice came down to him amplified by the echo :

"I'm getting soaked, and there's such a draught I don't think I'll manage to get anything out of this flare."

The small light on the front of Loubens's helmet was still spinning round, and Tazieff, patient or stubborn, rather, was waiting for the lucky moment and thinking, " If it doesn't come, I'll press the button all the same. Perhaps that point of light moving in space will give a curious effect."

Intent on finding the best angle, he did not immediately grasp what was happening when he saw the light rushing towards him and an anguished cry beat against his ears.

What had happened?

The clamp—there was only *one*—which closed the eye at the end of the cable had just given way, and the man whose life depended on it plunged down towards the chaos of rocks which formed the cone-shaped pile of rubble. His body passed a yard or two from where Tazieff was standing, but after striking the bottom it rolled on down the rocks. Labeyrie rushed forward to stop it and put an end to this fearful fall.

THE RACE WITH DEATH

" Hullo, winch . . . Hullo, winch . . . Hullo, winch. . . ."

It was a relief to the men up top to hear this voice from down below. Not knowing what had happened, but guessing that something was wrong, Cosyns had eased the cable off immediately after Loubens's fall, and from that moment the surface party waited. In the long hour that followed—and they waited a full hour—they imagined all kinds of things. The very idea that the device to which they had all entrusted their lives and which they were willing to trust again had failed one of them occurred to nobody. When Labeyrie spoke at last and said, " Loubens has fallen and is seriously hurt," those tragic words, all the more tragic because they were terse, brief, without fuss, brought no reply. Labeyrie had to repeat them, and only then did the full horror of the situation dawn on those who had gathered round the *doline*.

" Mairey, Mairey," called Cosyns in a hollow voice, unaware that the doctor was standing beside him.

Mairey quickly seized the earphones, and questions and

answers were rapidly exchanged, reduced to bare essentials.
" How is he?"
" Unconscious."
" How long?"
" From the first."
" His breathing?"
" Violent, fifty-eight times a minute."
" What's his condition."
" There's froth round his mouth; I think his upper jaw is broken, but I'm not sure, and there is probably something wrong with his back too, for though he's unconscious he keeps holding his hand to his side."
" Where have you put him?"
" He's near our camp, sheltered from falling stones. We've taken his helmet off—nothing abnormal there. The helmet has stood up to it, thanks to the glass, and I don't think we need fear a fractured skull. We moved him as gently as we could on a tent canvas. We had to move him twenty yards and it took us half an hour."

He didn't mention that Beppo Occhialini, who was asleep in the tent at the time of the accident had not stopped to put anything on his feet and had rushed up barefoot, regardless of pneumonia.

All Labeyrie asked was:
" What should we do?"
" Keep him absolutely still somewhere firm and level."
" Right."
" I'll come down as soon as it's possible."
Mairey handed the telephone to Lévi.
" We'll do all we can to bring him up, believe me. Do you think he will last a few hours or not?"
Labeyrie did not reply and Lévi went on:
" Can you hear me? Do you think there's any chance of using rope ladders?"
" No, it's quite impossible. Loubens has no proper protection. Stones are bound to fall on him, and he wouldn't have a chance. Raise the cable, repair it, and send Mairey down as quick as you can."

No more was said, and while Occhialini, Tazieff and Labeyrie began their long vigil with Loubens fighting for his life beside them, the surface party were busy organising help. Pierre Louis began repairing the winch and strengthening it; Lévi got in touch with the authorities and roused the whole country; Cosyns, shattered by the blow, tried to pull himself together, and Casteret got to work on the problem of how to bring Loubens up.

The whole camp was anxious and distressed. Disconsolate groups gathered at the edge of the *doline* or over by the tents and shepherds' huts. Two of the shepherds had gone to rescue a dog that had fallen into a nearby hole, and they were being helped by the five Lyons scouts—Georges and Louis Ballandreaux, Michel Letrône, and Daniel and Georges Epelly—who were expert in making descents with rope ladders, and who a few days before had broken the world record for this kind of work in the Fertel pot-hole, which was also in the " Gruyère cheese." They did not belong to Cosyns's expedition but they were in close touch with it, and when they learnt that there had been a serious accident at the bottom of Pierre Saint-Martin, they at once left their own work to come and help.

It was evening before the tension eased. Towards eight o'clock the noise of an engine broke the silence on the mountainside and the news spread like a trail of gunpowder that a Junkers was flying over the area. Hopes rose, wild and unreasoning, and those who were watching began to run, waving excitedly to the plane which brought help from the sky.

This was how Casteret described it:

" I shall never forget the plane from the air force base at Pau which flew over us at dusk in answer to a radio message. It came skimming over the mountain ridges, just as they were being swept by a violent storm which tore our tents down. In spite of these dangerous conditions the pilot managed to drop a special stretcher and medical supplies to us."

" It was a majestic sight," he added, " to watch the airmen

braving the storm to bring help to those who were trying to save a man's life deep down in the bowels of the earth."

Help was really on its way and the whole camp was moved by a spirit of human kindness. The feeling of helplessness in the face of disaster vanished, the cable was repaired and Mairey got ready to go down with medical supplies and the stretcher. Other planes were expected and the Lyons scouts with some of the shepherds were on their way to the *doline* bringing their cumbrous equipment with them. People were hurrying to Pierre Saint-Martin from the nearby villages and from the houses in the valley. If there was a chance of saving Loubens, it would be exploited to the full.

There was another painful moment when Mairey stood at the entrance to the shaft with his harness on. He was badly handicapped by the awkwardness of the stretcher, and this immeasurably increased the difficulties of the descent; not only that, but he was, of course, the first man since the accident to entrust his life to a machine which had let them down once already.

Lévi stood close by him, desperately anxious, but doing all he could to hide his very natural feelings and keep a grip upon himself.

" Doc," he said, putting a hand on Mairey's shoulder, " you must have confidence in those clamps."

To which Mairey replied, speaking very slowly : " I have no confidence in them at all." Then, without another word, he lowered himself resolutely into the mouth of the hole and vanished from sight, whilst the others watched anxiously. When he reached the bottom, Tazieff, Occhialini and Labeyrie had already been waiting helplessly at Loubens's side for fifteen hours.

POWERLESS TO HELP

It is agonising, waiting for help that can never come fast enough and knowing nothing of what is going on. You alternate between wild hope and deep despair—you build

on senseless fancies. Those at the surface knew this all too
well. But to be beyond the reach of the rest of the world,
powerless to help a friend who is at the point of death,
unable even to relieve his sufferings, is more than agonising;
it soon becomes unendurable. But the three men who waited
at the bottom of the shaft could do nothing but get used to
it. " If only Mairey gets here soon," they kept saying as they
paced to and fro. " If only Marcel stays unconscious until
he comes." They thought with horror of his regaining consciousness, screaming in agony at the sudden rush of pain
through his injured body, and not a soul being able to help
him.

There was no chance of killing time by hanging on the
telephone. It no longer answered; their separation from the
world of the living could not be more complete.

" Good God, what on earth are they doing up top?" At
times they would stamp the ground with their feet, grown
men though they were, whose courage and strength of nerve
no one would deny.

Then Labeyrie or Tazieff would say, as the sound of the
injured man gasping for breath pursued them as in a night-
mare: " The strength he must be losing by having to breathe
like that all the time! It's amazing how tough a man can be.
If only we could get him to drink something." But they knew
this was impossible. His mouth was now full of mucus and
the slightest drop of any kind of liquid could easily choke
him. Still—they had to kill the wild fears that haunted them;
better to talk nonsense than to stay silent.

After a while they had a meal, and then lay down to try to
sleep, but there was no hope of rest with that heart-rending
sound of a man gasping for breath a few feet away. They
cursed the men who worked up top with a freedom they
would never have believed themselves capable of.

There was a moment of panic later on, and it was
Occhialini who caused it.

" Tazieff," he cried suddenly; it was almost a groan, and
seizing the photographer's arm roughly he asked: " Do you
remember how the Spaniards behaved?"

"What do you mean?"

"You know, when they came up to the camp near the *doline*, were they friendly?"

"What makes you ask? What are you worrying about the carabineers for?"

"It's not that, but suppose there had been a quarrel, and that made the delicate situation caused by the accident still worse."

"And now the Spaniards have driven everyone away? Or clapped them all in jug?" jeered Labeyrie. "No, my lad, things like that just don't happen."

But Occhialini was not reassured, and to tell the truth, neither Tazieff nor even Labeyrie, for all his fine logic, could rid themselves of a vague feeling of apprehension.

"No, it's absurd," the young scientist muttered. "I took a good look at those soldiers. They had decent faces, and at a time like this Madrid would not intervene in such an unfriendly way."

It needed some new development to make them forget their childish fears. Occhialini had bent over Loubens, and was looking at him with renewed concern. The others came over. There was no more froth coming from Loubens's mouth, but only from his nose. The infection was rising.

Hour after hour went by and still they waited. Gradually the three men moved closer together, seeking a little bodily warmth. They felt their limbs growing numb, and their minds, too. They became light-headed, their brains went limp, they felt like automatons, and they were long past the stage of hovering between hope and despair. At least they thought so, but suddenly Labeyrie saw the cable begin to jerk, and when he realised that it was all over, that interminable, inhuman vigil, all his strength and mental energy flowed back again, and he shook the others.

"Someone's coming down," he shouted. "Mairey's coming down. They've not forgotten us."

The next moment the three men were on their feet busily winding the cable round the reel as it came down, and then Occhialini thought of putting some water on to boil. When

Mairey emerged into the vault, and his lamp began to spin round at just the spot where Loubens had fallen from the cable, Labeyrie had to shut his eyes for a brief moment. He was well aware that he was in the grip of a violent rush of feeling, which he would not be able to master very easily. But he was strong-willed by nature, and he began at once to fight it. As Mairey reached the bottom, he rushed towards him and helped to relieve him of the stretcher and his haversack.

Mairey went over to the injured man at once.

" Well?" asked Tazieff impatiently as the examination went on a long time. " There's no hope?"

The doctor hesitated, unable to hide his anxiety. Labeyrie and Occhialini asked the same question, but they knew the answer already. When Mairey spoke the four short words, " He is done for," they were shocked, naturally, but not with the violence of hope betrayed, which can drive men mad.

" Why?" Labeyrie spoke harshly. " His skull is not broken."

" It is. His skull is broken and his spine, too."

He looked up towards the shaft. " Can you imagine an injured man being taken up there with a broken spine?"

" Yet he moved his legs and there was no bleeding from his ears."

" He's been bleeding from his nose and that's not injured."

He decided that it was useless to say any more. He turned to his haversack and quietly took out his surgical instruments. Anyone who did not know Mairey would have thought then that he was devoid of all feeling. His actions were precise, his face impassive. But it was no more than a natural reserve in the presence of others. On his way down the shaft with the stretcher Mairey had wept so bitterly that it was noticeable over the telephone when he spoke to the surface.

" All the same," he said, when he had examined his instruments, " we shall do all we possibly can for him. If there's a chance, no matter how small, we must see that he has it."

Then Tazieff burst out : " It's absurd. It's ridiculous to give up hope like this. Listen, I fell about thirty feet once myself on the cliffs of the Meuse in Belgium. Thirty feet, you hear! Almost as far as Marcel. And I fell badly, flat on my back, and it was no soft spot either—just about as hard as iron. I thought I was done for, but do you know what it cost me in the end? A small hole in my arm and a bruised back. What do you say to that?"

"Well," replied Mairey gently, "it only means that no two falls are alike. This time it's serious. Very serious."

A UNIQUE FEAT

Once the doctor had given his injections, they began to discuss the chances of getting Loubens to the surface. Occhialini was pessimistic.

"It's impossible," he said. "You say, doc, that the least movement might be fatal, and yet you want to take him up twelve hundred feet."

"If we strap him securely to the stretcher," Mairey said, "so that there is no possibility of his moving at all, we should be able to get him to the top alive. As for saving him down here, it's out of the question. He must open his eyes in a clean white hospital ward with all the latest modern equipment. You dare to compare this cave with that?"

They all glanced at the blackness around them, and Mairey went on: "I've made up my mind and I take full responsibility. We'll let him rest here for a little while first, and then we'll strap him to the stretcher. That won't be easy. It may take hours, and it may all be for nothing. But we must try."

There was a sound of falling stones just then, but they paid little attention. When it happened again shortly afterwards, and much louder this time, all except Mairey looked up in surprise.

"It's nothing," said Mairey, 'if you can call the racket the Lyons scouts are making in the shaft nothing."

They looked at him in astonishment.

" Yes," said Mairey, " the scouts had their ladders down a nearby pot-hole rescuing a shepherd's dog, when the news of the accident reached them. They gathered their equipment up at once and rushed over to the camp to help."

" Will they dare to come down here with rope ladders?" Tazieff asked. " With *rope ladders*?"

" Yes."

" But it's suicide. They don't realise . . ."

" I don't know about that," said Mairey. " They know what they are doing and they have plenty of courage."

" That's true enough," said Occhialini. " I saw them going down the Fertel pot-hole. It was absolutely amazing. Distances that would take us a good half-hour on their ladders, they did in fifteen minutes."

He was not exaggerating. Up above, Ballandreaux and his friends were causing quite a sensation. Casteret had said " No," at first. " No, it's very good of you, but it's far too dangerous. One casualty is enough. I don't want your deaths on my conscience." But they insisted, so forcibly and so persistently that Casteret gave way, partly because, knowing the shaft as well as he did, he was wondering how the stretcher and the man in it could ever be brought up. The only hope was to station men the whole length of the shaft to prevent the stretcher knocking against the rock face and to guide it past the ledges. Without a word, he seized one of the ladders and began to examine it with the greatest care.

The way the scouts put their ladders in position won everyone's admiration. Talk of monkeys and conjurers! That's exactly what they were—cave conjurers. When someone asked Ballandreaux how he acquired such agility and achieved such an astonishing victory over nature, he answered modestly, " There's nothing to it. Just constant practice."

They divided the operation up between them, placing two men at 260 feet, one at 390 and one at 785, and so the noise they made could be heard as clearly at the top as at the bottom. They formed a living, active, moving link between Cosyns, Casteret, Lévi and those with them at the surface

and the four men down below. Stones were whistling down
the shaft faster and more frequently and they burst against
the cone-shaped pile of rubble with a noise like that of gun-
fire. Sometimes, during a lull, the sound of orders being
given reached those who were waiting up top and those
down in the Lépineux cave.

Stationed on the narrow ledges the scouts drove their
pitons deep into the cracks in the wall of the shaft, then
hanging on to them by a loop of rope they took the next
piton, drove it in and so went down yard by yard. They
gave their instructions by blasts on their whistles, not by
microphone, and so they were all able to control the speed
of their descent: one blast meant stop, two blasts, up; three,
down. So it went on.

To the four men down below with Loubens it seemed
that the relief team would literally drop on top of them, and
the Lyons scouts were making it all seem so easy that it was
quite an effort to keep in mind the innumerable difficulties
which anyone coming down the Pierre Saint-Martin chimney
had to contend with.

"They're wonderful," murmured Occhialini. "Quite
amazing."

Mairey was busy all this time. He had drilled two small
holes into a helmet and threaded a piece of wire through
them to prevent Loubens's head being shaken during the
ascent. When the injured man was placed on the stretcher,
all that would be necessary would be to fasten the wire; and
to make him more comfortable he had fixed a length of
wood, hollowed out just where the head would rest. He had
also given a blood transfusion.

While Labeyrie and Occhialini were helping Mairey,
Tazieff seized the opportunity of going to the telephone for
news. "Hullo, winch," he said. Janssens was on watch and
answered, "I can hear you clearly." "Are you ready up
there?" "Yes, everything's ready, and as soon as the last
scout is in position we shall be able to start." "Good, we're
all ready here, too."

Tazieff went back to the camp, but as he came up to the

others he felt there was something odd and stopped dead. What was it? He thought a moment, and was alarmed to find nothing, or nothing unusual at all events. Everything seemed the same as before—the rocks precariously balanced, the monotonous sound of water dripping, the others moving quietly round Loubens. Then it dawned on him. Marcel. Yes, Marcel. There was a change in the injured man. His breathing was weaker—that was it—that jerky, violent breathing which had obsessed them all for the last thirty hours was losing its strength.

When he reached the others, Mairey told him to go back to the telephone and ask that the ascent should start at once.

"We've got to hurry," he said.

The men at the bottom were at the end of their tether, numb with cold, strain and exhaustion. The oil stove was burning and water was bubbling gently on the flame, but even that could not cheer them with thoughts of pleasanter things.

Loubens groaned—for the first time since he had been in a coma; they looked up slowly but only Mairey bent over the injured man. There was a second groan, then a third. What was happening? No one dared to move.

While the seconds passed and the doctor stretched out a hand towards Loubens's eyes, as he lay there silent now, the three men still did not move. They seemed turned to stone.

Labeyrie was the first to rouse himself; he rose and went over to the telephone.

"Hullo, winch." The words rose once again towards the light.

"Yes," came the answer.

"Marcel Loubens died five minutes ago."

Labeyrie put the headphones down. That was all. No more, no empty phrases, no display of emotion. The Lyons scouts stopped at once, and the men down below, worn out by thirty-six hours of struggle, hope and fear—Loubens had been fighting all that time—went back to the tent and fell asleep almost at once.

They felt nothing as yet, being too close to what had happened. Grief would come tomorrow, when they woke. Only then would their tears flow for their friend, who was dead. Only then would Labeyrie take an acetylene lamp and go up to the rock to write there in letters of smoke these very simple words:

HERE

MARCEL LOUBENS

LIVED

THE LAST DAYS OF HIS

COURAGEOUS LIFE

THE NEXT DAY

Marcel Loubens died at a quarter to eleven at night. Next morning at nine, Mairey left the camp to find a suitable place for burial, for no one then thought of taking the body to the surface; it would obviously be too dangerous, and though it was conceivable to risk life to save another's, and everything had been done to bring Loubens up while still alive, it would be madness to do so once he was dead. Furthermore, all the members of the expedition felt that the Lépineux cave was a fitting grave for one who had explored the depths of the earth.

Loubens himself had said as much to a friend one day when they were climbing the track which led from Sainte-Engrâce to Pierre Saint-Martin. " If I'm unlucky enough to have a serious accident at the bottom of a cave I cannot imagine a more suitable grave for a keen spelaeologist like myself than one of those dark, damp, uncomfortable, majestic caves."

He was laughing as he spoke, happy to be thirty, happy to be alive, happy to be on this mountain, where his optimism and faith enabled him to see men better than they really were, while feeling himself close to his Creator. Now he lay in the tranquil sleep of eternity, the sleep of a good and just man, in surroundings of impressive grandeur which spoke compellingly of God. What a sorry exchange it would be to take him from this mausoleum without equal anywhere in the world, and bury him in the soil of some village cemetery, where sooner or later his body would be attacked by the worms.

Madame Loubens, who was always with the men of Pierre Saint-Martin in thought, had been consulted and agreed with them. Only the simple heart of his aged mother, prostrate with grief, could not understand, and she asked at once if there was not some means of bringing her son up from the cave.

The first answer was that it could not be done.

Mairey, meanwhile, left problems like these to take care of themselves. For the moment first things must come first and the most urgent of all was to find in this chaos of rocks a fitting place for Loubens's body. He moved slowly, stumbling more than usual through nervous exhaustion, until he came to a kind of natural hollow between two slabs of stone. " Here he may rest," he said to himself. The place lay between the bivouac and the base camp, and it was not an easy matter to move the body, which was now laid out on the stretcher.

" The burial was very hard work," Tazieff says, " and almost the whole day went by without our noticing it. We laid his body in the hollow of a natural grave between two blocks of stone. He was now lying stiffly in a waterproof overall, parachute harness with shining buckles and straps, and glossy white helmet. It looked like a suit of armour. His left arm lay in plaster, stretched out beside him, his right was folded across his breast. His face, always so full of energy, took on in death a quiet nobility, like a medieval effigy, a knight dead but unconquered."

There is no earth to be found in the Lépineux cave, and they had therefore to cover Loubens with a fine gravel which they collected in their helmets. When this was done, they used a coarser gravel, and then after one or two layers of that they changed to stones, choosing bigger and bigger ones as they went along. At the end of the day Labeyrie carved an epitaph and Tazieff made a cross out of rectangular pieces of sheet iron covered with luminous white paint and laid it on a sloping stone. When anyone came down the shaft, his lamp was bound to light up the cross as soon as he reached the vault of the vast Lépineux cave.

Labeyrie was the first to return to the surface. The accident had increased his natural caution, and he and the others spent several hours examining his gear and the end of the cable. Without a moment's hesitation he cut several lengths of valuable nylon rope to make additional straps.

"What a pity," groaned Tazieff. "Half-inch nylon and brand new!"

Labeyrie was unabashed. "Well, what of it? I mean to get out alive." Tazieff knew what he meant only too well; so well, in fact, that when Labeyrie reached the fatal height, he was obliged to shut his eyes, in spite of the additional precautions that had been taken. He saw Loubens falling as if it were happening a second time, and his dread of the accident which could always happen only passed when Labeyrie had entered the shaft itself.

Occhialini went up next early in the afternoon, and Tazieff stayed with Mairey. Again he had to look away when the Italian reached the height at which the clamp had given way. Mairey watched him curiously, not understanding this nervous reaction, because he had not been there when the accident happened. Once alone, they looked at each other without saying anything, but they read each other's thoughts plainly enough. What was left unsaid was that since they were there, both of them strong and determined, there was no reason why they should not go back to the cave which Labeyrie had thought so small, and Loubens so large.

A little later Tazieff spoke his thoughts aloud: "You see, André, it would be wonderful if we could prove him right."

The doctor felt the same, and about four o'clock they called the surface. "Hullo, winch. We are all in. There's no question of our coming up today. We're going to sleep. Don't expect to hear from us before two o'clock tomorrow. Is that all right?'

It was just what they wanted up top, and permission was promptly given.

They then did exactly as they had said; dead beat, they undressed, got into the tent and their sleeping bags, and slept the deep sleep of those who return to a comfortable bed after enduring hardships worthy of the fakirs. But next morning they were up at eight, washed quickly, swallowed a whole bottle of malt extract, and at nine exactly they left the camp for the Elizabeth Casteret cave.

They made a good pace from the start. Both were tough and seasoned explorers and they knew this part of the hole well enough to enter it light-heartedly. They rounded " Gibraltar " without difficulty and reached the shaft down to the Casteret cave in record time. Tazieff slid to the bottom as fast as the sixty feet or so of nylon rope would uncoil, and Mairey followed him without any hesitation. They crossed the cave diagonally in the direction of the spot where the torrent vanished, and arrived at the entrance to the cave which Loubens had reached a few days before, without meeting any difficulty. The floor sloped at an angle of about thirty degrees, and somewhere in the darkness they could hear the roar of the waterfall. They went down without slackening their pace, only to stop dead thirty feet lower down in front of a small pile of stones.

" We're on the right road," Mairey said. " They reached this far."

" Yes, but not beyond. The unknown starts here."

There was a trace of emotion in Tazieff's voice as he spoke. He raised his lamp towards the vault, but he could see no end to it. " Labeyrie seems to have been a little short-sighted," he said. There was no doubt about its size now, but Mairey and Tazieff were in the grip of " exploration fever " and they did not stop to argue about it. They left the cave behind them and made towards the sound of the water.

Mairey was the first to reach the torrent. " Wait for me

Left: the bivouac in the Lépineux cave

Right: the under-ground river— the farthest point reached in the explorations of 1954. It lies under Spanish soil.

Delteil stands on an enormous boulder at the bottom of the hole.

Lévi and Mairey stand in the La Verna cave, the deepest point so far reached in the Pierre Saint-Martin hole, and in 1953 a world record.

here a moment," he said to Tazieff, who had caught up with
him. " I'm going to skirt the edge of the stream and see if
there's a way through."

" There's a *siphon*," Mairey called a few seconds later.
" Shall we dive?"

Tazieff shivered. The idea of undressing and diving into
water with a temperature of forty degrees had no appeal for
him.

" Better try to find another way higher up."

Signposting their way as they went they reached
Loubens's cairn without difficulty. They branched off to the
left, and then suddenly came upon a sizeable opening half
way up the wall and only a few feet above their heads. It
led into a tiny cave, and this they crossed quickly. Beyond
it the going was easy and they found themselves back in the
great cave, vast in size and impenetrably dark.

" What about lighting a flare," Mairey suggested. " I know
you've almost used up your reserves, but I feel it's a moment
to be extravagant. It's so stupendous."

Tazieff agreed, and unpacking his camera he handed
Mairey a magnesium flare, and asked him to go as far away
as he could.

" Try and get the light on the rocks," he asked.

Seconds later, in a fleeting moment of wonder, the light
let them see the true dimensions of the cave in which they
stood. It was like a fantastic ship—fantastic is the word, as
Loubens had said in his Toulouse accent—and it lost nothing
in comparison with the two caves that went before it; in fact,
it was without question the largest of the three caves so far
known.

" Mairey! Hey, Mairey! Where are you?"

He had vanished, but not far, and Tazieff heard him reply
at once. " It's all right. Let me scout around a bit. It's
amazing, absolutely amazing." It was a quarter of an hour
before the doctor had quenched his thirst for discovery and
Tazieff could finish what he wanted to say.

" What do you think?" he said quietly. " Shall we call this
the Loubens cave?"

" Need you ask? Of course we will." And off he went again into the unknown.

" André! Wait for me."

But there was no answer. " I could see," wrote Tazieff, " two or three shafts of light pointing towards the roof, where it dropped towards the floor some fifty yards farther on. That was the end of the cave. Where had André vanished to now? I rushed on, jumping from boulder to boulder, all my energy restored. Then I saw what it was. Where the cave came to an end, a tunnel opened right at the bottom, a black, yawning tunnel. The fluorescent strips which Mairey had dropped led me to it."

Tazieff was seeing for the first time what the others were later to call the " Métro."

" I made my way into the tunnel," he went on. " It was on the same scale as the cave I had just left—thirty feet high and sixty to a hundred and twenty feet wide. I looked at the time, and at the altimeter, and wrote my observations down in my notebook, which was now soaked. Then I followed Mairey as fast as I could.

" The tunnel ran in a dead straight line north-west, and was big enough to take half a dozen trains running abreast. It dropped at an angle of only a few degrees in contrast to the steep slope in the other caves. There was no water on the floor, nothing but large boulders piled one on top of another.

" ' Hulloo-oo!' I was glad to hear Mairey calling, and to find him again and share his strange impressions. He was waiting for me two hundred yards inside the tunnel. ' Come here and listen,' he said as I came up to him.

" I listened for a moment. A great roaring sound filled the cave. It was tremendously impressive. Where did it come from? We had to listen very carefully to be sure, because the rumbling seemed to come from everywhere at once; in fact, it came from down below.

" ' The river,' André said.

" We started off again with the tunnel getting no smaller. A little farther on the water reappeared among the boulders

strewn along the floor, and in a few steps we passed from a
dry gallery on to the banks of a large subterranean river, a
much larger river than the streams we were familiar with
up to now; four to five times the volume of water, fifteen to
twenty feet wide and up to six feet deep. We went on
quickly, impatient to know more about it and with an eye
on the time we should have to turn back.

" Sometimes the going was easy, but we came to some
ticklish places where we had to jump across the crystal-clear
water—so clear, in fact, that I twice saw what I thought to
be a good foothold on a rock only to get wet up to the ankles,
through not realising that my stepping stone lay under the
surface of the water.

" At twelve forty-five, when we had been going along this
amazing tunnel for half an hour in a dead straight line, we
stopped at the edge of a large pool of still water, slightly
greenish in colour. We probed the darkness beyond this
little lake with our lamps only to find that the tunnel seemed
to go on indefinitely. I lit one of our last magnesium flares
and took several yards of film, while André made use of the
light to examine the gallery. The tunnel went on just the
same for as far as he could see."

In circumstances like these it was a big sacrifice to have
to turn back, but it was getting late and there was no point
in causing the men up top needless anxiety.

" All the same . . ." Mairey said, without finishing his
sentence. " All the same . . ." There was no need for him
to go on. Both men shared the same thought, that if they
went on they would eventually reach the end of the galleries
and of the caves and come out into the open air four
thousand feet lower down either in the Arette valley or in
the Sainte-Engrâce valley. " All the same . . ." Tazieff said
sadly, mechanically repeating what the doctor had said.

The return journey was tedious enough. Doped with
benzedrine and exhausted after six hours walking over rocks
which did not exactly make for easy going, they missed their
way, and at one time had to admit that they would never
find it again.

"Are you sure we're still in the Casteret cave?" Tazieff asked suddenly.

Mairey had to reassure him, and to do so he had to bring all his powers of persuasion to bear. But his arguments were in any case of little use. Tazieff suddenly collapsed on the rocks as though he were drunk and when he tried to get up again he found to his annoyance that he had cramp in his legs and could not stand up, and he had to crawl along on his hands and knees.

"I feel such a fool," he complained. "I could cry with shame."

Mairey could do nothing to help him, being too busy searching for the way out, which meant finding the shaft and recognising it from the bottom this time and not from the top. "To think," he said to himself, "that Loubens was wandering about here all alone. He certainly had pluck."

Mairey made two fruitless attempts and had to come back again, but the third time he was lucky, and found the rope ladder hanging against the rock, pointing the way out.

"Haroun," he shouted. "You can breathe again. We're saved."

Tazieff massaged his legs for a good ten minutes before he attempted to climb the ladder. The rungs were only six inches wide, and so it was not exactly a nice easy way up.

*   *   *   *   *

Their last act before finally leaving the hole for that year was to lay on Loubens's grave some flowers which Occhialini had brought down as a tribute from Madame Labeyrie. They had been five days on the way, but they were still remarkably fresh; and Casteret who made the first descent next year found them almost intact.

Tazieff was the first to go up, but though he left the bottom at five in the afternoon, he only reached the surface at half past nine, after an agonising stop two hundred feet up, from where he could still see Mairey's lamp moving in the depths of the Lépineux cave.

Everyone up top had to help to bring him up. The winch

refused to work once again and spelaeologists, shepherds, gendarmes, carabineers and reporters were all called in to haul on the cable. When Tazieff emerged at last, he looked more like something which had been fished out of the Seine than a spelaeologist. He had forgotten to put on his waterproof overalls, and for four hours water had been pouring over his shoulders and down his back. He dropped heavily to the ground at their feet. " Quick," he groaned, " send the rope down to Mairey, quick. It's pretty tough, you know, waiting down there."

Unfortunately there was more trouble with the winch, and the doctor had to spend the night at the bottom, alone with the dead man. He was not brought up until next day, when the sun was already high.

So ended this dramatic week-end.

Chapter Six

1951

AS FAR AS THE CASTERET CAVE

TH E year 1951 seems quiet in comparison with the
excitement of the three years that followed. There was
drama in 1952, 1953 and 1954, the fever of discovery
ran high and Pierre Saint-Martin became famous; but it was
in 1951 all the same that the first descents were made and
exploration brought its first rewards.

"I'm happy." Those were Georges Lépineux's words as
he greeted Haroun Tazieff, who was waiting for him at the
260-feet ledge. Lépineux had discovered the pot-hole, had
been the first to go down, had just broken the world record
for the deepest descent, and was now on his way up,
exhausted but triumphant.

For the members of the expedition, and particularly for
those who knew Loubens and how the La Verna cave had
been discovered, all that seems long past, and now that
everybody has heard of the wonders that lie hidden beneath
Pierre Saint-Martin, it may seem naïve to enthuse about this
first descent and to echo those early cries of triumph. In
those days they had only just begun to move cautiously
across the Casteret cave, the second to be discovered, which
you might almost say is now crossed at the double.

In 1951 there were fewer reporters than there were in the
following years, and a mere handful of cameramen and
tourists. Little was reported in the newspapers. The expedition was left to itself on a mountain top where only shepherds lived, and the world took no notice of it.

Tazieff was describing his exploration of the Stromboli crater and how it was belching fire within forty yards of him. He had left it only three weeks before in order to join the team at Pierre Saint-Martin. Loubens and Labeyrie were listening eagerly, interrupting him now and then in their strong Midi accents. Lépineux was getting ready to go down the shaft, and Cosyns and Janssens were working the winch, a modest pedal winch, where the motive power was human energy.

An atmosphere like that cannot be recreated today. If there is another expedition in the summer of 1955 it will be along the lines of those of 1953 and 1954. Everyone will be talking about it and it will attract a great many spectators. It is like a play where you know the story; it can only repeat itself. The expeditions of 1952 to 1955, which we may as well include, form a whole, and we can jump from one to another without feeling lost. The 1951 expedition belongs irrevocably to the past.

AT THE TOP OF THE SHAFT

It was in 1950, you remember, that Cosyns and his party dropped a sounding line into a pot-hole which was then unknown. When this disclosed a shaft of considerable depth, a second test—or rather a check—was made with a balloon, and what was left of the team at Pierre Saint-Martin at the end of the holiday had to accept the general belief that the depth of the shaft was eleven hundred feet.

In the spring of 1951, a number of spelaeologists belonging to the group met to discuss, for obvious reasons, the plans for the next expedition. Rope ladders were rejected as impracticable, and a steel cable worked by a powerful winch was proposed, and that was why Cosyns arrived with a kind of bicycle, which took a week to set up at the edge of the *doline*.

Everything still remained to be done. A wild unfriendly

place had to be transformed, not perhaps into a workshop exactly, but at least into somewhere accessible. In 1951 the entrance to the pot-hole was not anything like as large as it became later; it was just an ordinary hole in the friable rock, and the ceiling itself was a constant danger, consisting of crumbling stone and overhanging rock which was riddled with cracks. It took the team two full days to deal with this danger by filling the cracks with mortar and building a kind of artificial ledge, with the object of increasing the flow of fresh air into the damp atmosphere of the caves below. This wasted two whole days and the first descent did not take place until the eighth day. Everything had to be planned down to the last detail before launching an attack upon the unknown, with a day for trials, a day for testing the winch, and days of just waiting for the weather to turn fine— because rain and mists are more frequent up there than the sun you see on picture postcards.

The eighth day was just right, and they could get started. Tazieff took up his position at point 260, where he stayed motionless for seven hours, being afraid that the slightest movement might start a fall of stones, which was something to be avoided as Lépineux was acting as chimney-sweep below him. On his way back Lépineux stopped a moment on Tazieff's ledge. He was jubilant, as we already know, over what he had seen. "It's vast down there," he told Tazieff. "There's a cave big enough to hold Notre Dame Cathedral." But his excitement was nothing to what it would have been if he had known that there were several other caves which would take Notre Dame, and that all of these were lower down the same hole, which was soon to bear his name.

Lépineux returned to the surface so that Jackie Erthaud could go down, and afterwards it was Tazieff's turn. Erthaud had already gone up again and Tazieff was alone waiting for Loubens to arrive, before setting off with him to explore all that could be explored.

Loubens's descent was a joy. Going down for the first time into the deepest hole in the world, which was later to be his grave, he had no inkling of the pathos of it all. Tazieff, who was talking to him over the microphone, has described the sort of remarks this boy from Toulouse would make.

"His voice came nearer, and presently I caught what he was saying and his rich Gascon accent. 'Yes, I'm all right. I'm window gazing. It's smooth as glass and I'm right on top of it.' I waited a moment and then I called him. 'Hullo, Loubens.' 'Hullo, Tazieff. I'm fed up. Is it still far to where you are?' 'I can't see you, but you should soon be reaching the top of the cave.' 'Is your lamp alight?' 'Yes.' Then a little later, 'Hullo, Tazieff. I can see your light at last. Good Heavens, what a spin!'"

Tazieff, for his part, could see what looked like a puppet spinning in space, legs apart and hands clasped to his stomach, a puppet without a face which was almost entirely covered by a large helmet. As he touched the ground, the puppet turned into a balloon, dangling from the end of his rope and rebounding from rock to rock with the grace of an elephant. "Oh, dear," he said, "how sore your sides get." At the third metamorphosis, the balloon became a man, and Loubens took off his harness.

"Have you any idea how to put all this stuff on again," he asked Tazieff, as they went over to the bivouac.

"Not much. But I've got the general idea, all the same. The important thing is to fasten the buckles so that they don't open on the way down."

"No," murmured Loubens. "But if that should happen, look after Patrick for me."

Thinking this a little over-dramatic, he suddenly remembered that Tazieff himself had only just come down a pothole for the first time in his life.

"Well," he said, "what do you think of it?"

Tazieff snorted. "Do you mean to tell me you come down into these caves of yours each year for the *fun* of it?"

They had a meal—biscuits, vitamin spread and chocolate —which reminded him of his remark about the fun of it. "For the *fun* of it," he queried, and grimaced. Those scientific sorts of food were not much to his taste; what he wanted

was a piece of bread and a hunk of cheese and the glass of
red wine which could be had anywhere up top.

But it was no good brooding about life up there, because
they were not going up again just yet. Before that happened,
there was a hole to be explored, which meant a slow and
painful journey over rocks lying at all kinds of angles.

They started off after telling Lévi not to worry about them
again that night. " We'll contact you tomorrow morning at
six. Not before."

THE FIRST DISCOVERIES

Loubens's first discovery was a fissure and he set off along
it at such a pace that he disappeared out of Tazieff's sight
almost immediately. It opened on to a passage which shot
off at an angle, and he soon returned.

" Well, is there a way through?" Tazieff asked.

" I don't think so. I could hear water, quite definitely
water and not wind."

" Then there should be more caves still after this one?"

" No doubt about it," said Loubens, " but we have got to
find a way through. If we can't do that, there can be a
hundred caves and we still won't get anywhere."

This time they both tried to find a means of getting out of
the first cave. They made their way between giant boulders,
some of which were twenty-five feet high like a two-storey
house, and after climbing up one side and sliding down the
other, they at last found a hole, six feet by three. They bent
down and saw, ten feet below, a ledge of loose stones,
beyond which stretched an open space.

Loubens whistled. " Not bad, not bad at all," he said.

He cleared the entrance to the opening, uncoiled a rope
and dropped down on to the ledge with a grin of delight,
and then disappeared as soon as he had taken his bearings.

" Well?" shouted Tazieff, who was still holding the rope at
the top of the hole.

"Well, I rather think that if I go another inch all these stones will give way, and I'll end up Lord knows where. It's a colossal slope of fallen stones, and they're all crumbling."

A little later came the bald announcement:

"It's frightening."

Tazieff thought that he was going to come up again, but he did not know his man. Loubens, the hero of the Henne-Morte pot-hole, was not the man to stop exploring through lack of courage. He stated the bare fact and no more, because he had good reason to be afraid, but then he went on:

"Pass me down the ladder."

Tazieff unrolled what spelaeologists call an "electron ladder," which has hollow tubes made out of light alloy instead of wooden rungs and they are joined together by steel wire instead of rope, and the whole thing looks as though it has been made by spiders.

Loubens climbed on to it carefully.

"Shall I wait for you here?" Tazieff asked.

There was no reply from Loubens, and it was minutes before he shouted back:

"No, I can't get this way. I don't know why it's not all given way under my weight—it's just a house of cards."

They folded the ladder up again, put the rope back in the haversack, and made their way home to the bivouac, wondering if they would ever find a way out of the cave big enough for them to use. They felt more like getting into the tent and going to sleep than starting off again in search of it. It would all seem simple enough later on in 1952 and 1953, when the hole was no longer the large question mark it was now, but to Loubens and Tazieff it was one vast impenetrable darkness, with the floor a mass of stones dropping away at a dangerous angle and where the next step you took might hurl you into space and to a certain death.

They made a cup of hot coffee to cure the first signs of weariness and at about midnight they found another hole between two boulders, much like the first one but less exposed. Out came the rope and ladder again, and Loubens dropped down into it.

"Stop."

He had reached the bottom of the slope—its average angle was about thirty degrees—and this time he was well and truly inside a new cave.

What it amounted to was this, that at the end of the first cave, which is known as the Lépineux cave and where the shaft ends, the roof and the floor meet to form a wall with a number of gaps in it. Many of these were unlikely to prove passable, but others provided a way through which could be negotiated with a little difficulty. Loubens had now set off along one of these.

"Shall I follow?" Tazieff asked.

"No," called Loubens. "I would rather you stay where you are. It's wiser."

Tazieff had to content himself with listening to the sound of Loubens disappearing into the cave with shouts of "It's fantastic . . . It's fantastic . . ." This was the Elizabeth Casteret cave that Loubens was in the process of exploring, a vast chaotic labyrinth of rocks, where many a spelaeologist was still to get himself lost in the years to come, in spite of all the sign-posts that had been put up. Mairey lost his way in it for the fourth time in 1954.

There is no point in stressing Loubens's courage under conditions like these, and to say that he lost his way is just so many words. Tazieff, who had to stay where he was at the entrance to the shaft, was now to have the worst fright of his life underground.

"I could not hear him any longer, and my shouts went unanswered. Well, I thought, he must have gone behind one of those huge boulders. I'll be able to hear him again in a moment. Minutes went by, and the silence grew worse and worse. If he's not behind a boulder, perhaps he's in a side gallery. I kept singing out with a deep-throated 'Ho!'; then I listened, counted up to thirty and tried again. I had glanced at my watch when Loubens left me. I remembered it had said thirteen minutes past three. It was now five past

four. Four ten, four fifteen, four thirty. Would I have to take
care of Patrick? Twenty to five. I'm usually an optimist, but
my optimism was fading out like the lamp I had left on the
rock over there. I thought of a thousand possible accidents.
Five o'clock. What am I to do? If he had lost his way, I
should have heard his shouts. I wanted to go down myself,
not to explore, of course. But what chance would I have of
finding him in this enormous cave, and even if I found him,
what could I do? If he was dead, nothing; if he was hurt,
not very much, for I could never manage to get him back
here. What then?

"There was nothing I could do but wait. Wait and shout
from time to time, in case he had only lost his way. If there
was still nothing at half past five, I would go back to the
bivouac. We had arranged to call the surface at six o'clock
precisely. There would be nothing left to do but ask for help.
Labeyrie could come down, and Janssens, and the others.
They were all good chaps.

"I don't know whether I gave a start or not when I heard
Loubens shout again after an hour and a half's silence. It
came from a long way off. My answer was a whoop of joy.
Loubens's voice came nearer. 'Tazieff, where are you?'
'He-e-e-e-re!' 'Where's that?' 'Place Vendôme, you idiot.
Where do you think I am? At the entrance to the cave, of
course.' 'But I can hear you from all four sides at once—
there are echoes everywhere!'

"The only thing to do in the circumstances was to try one
direction after another, until we hit on the right one, and
that is what I told him to do. Then I made my shouts more
frequent, and lit one of my last magnesium flares. Loubens
tried one direction, then another. Then, all of a sudden,
close beside me I heard: 'Hullo! I can see your light. There
it is. I can recognise the slope. I'm dead beat, old boy.'

" 'What happened, you idiot? Why the silence?'

" 'I got lost—while I was taking notes and trying to work
out the distance covered. What a cave, old boy! It's a good
five hundred yards by three hundred. Can you imagine it?'

" 'And its height?' I asked.

" ' Three hundred feet.'

" ' What happens at the far end?'

" ' There's a river . . .' "

That was the gist of what Loubens said when he found Tazieff again. He was worn out by the tremendous exertion of exploring this second cave—beyond which he was never to go—and he dragged himself back to the bivouac. He was now the man to have penetrated farther than anyone into the bowels of the earth, and this coveted honour belonged to him for that year at least. Triumphant, but utterly exhausted, he began to sob.

Tazieff was the first to return to the surface, giving Loubens time to recover. But their feelings were mixed when they reached the top again. It had never occurred to them that they would not work another shift, and their disappointment was great when they learnt that the winch would not be working again.

"That will be for next year," Cosyns said. "We'll bring better equipment, and the winch will be driven by an electric motor. It's essential if we are to do anything worth while here."

It would be worth while, of course, but dangerous all the same. But Loubens did not give a thought to that. Tazieff and he knocked the Bouchets up at one in the morning and he called gaily to Mme Bouchet: "You won't mind making some of your excellent punch for a world record holder, will you, Mme Bouchet?"

Chapter Seven

THE OTHER CAVES

PIERRE SAINT-MARTIN is not the whole of
spelaeology. There are other important caves in France
and elsewhere, particularly in Switzerland, Austria,
Italy and Belgium, some untouched and others which are
explored each year by enthusiastic teams of spelaeologists.
Unfortunate accidents like that to Loubens, and several
others at Pierre Saint-Martin which did not prove fatal, have
also happened elsewhere, at Cigalère, Henne-Morte,
Katavothre de Taka in Greece, Lirou in the Hérault
department, Hohl-Loch in Switzerland, the Trou du Glaz,
La Grotte Norée in Poitiers, and in Wales.

It is not even certain that Pierre Saint-Martin is the
world's deepest pot-hole. We were certain it was in 1953 and
until 16 August 1954. But the following day a triumphant
announcement from Nice appeared in the newspapers:

" The spelaeological expedition at Mount Marguaris, in
the French-Italian Maritime Alps, finished work there on
Monday after three weeks of underground exploration, in
the course of which a cave was discovered 2,788 feet deep.

" The expedition, consisting of about forty members, was
led by Jacques Rouire and worked under the auspices of the
National Committee for Spelaeology.

" The explorations were carried out in three sections. Some
ten caves were explored in the Dupega valley in Italy, where
last year the outfalls of underground streams were revealed
by the use of fluorescein. One of these caves gave access to

a subterranean river which has its source between four and five thousand feet up in the Marguaris massif.

" At a medium altitude, the Piaggia-Bella cave, which was visited last year, has been re-explored and surveyed. An entrance to the lower galleries has been discovered, giving rise to the hope that an effective link-up will be made with the Dupega outfalls.

" Finally, at high altitudes of approximately eight thousand feet several pot-holes have been explored. One of them, the Raymond Gache, named after the president of the French Spelaeological Society, has been explored to a depth of 1,150 feet.

" It's link-up with the Piaggia-Bella cave is almost certain, but the late hour of its discovery made this impossible to effect. That will be undertaken in 1955.

" The difference of level between the entrance of the Gache pot-hole and the bottom of the Piaggia-Bella cave is of the order of 2,788 feet, which would easily make it the deepest cave in the world with the highest entrance in the world, that is over eight thousand feet.

" If, on the other hand, as is hoped, a link-up can be effected between Piaggia-Bella and the Dupega caves the total depth will amount to about 4,400 feet."

LA CIGALÈRE

All the same, it must be remembered that the Pierre Saint-Martin pot-hole has not been completely explored. In the opinion of the most experienced spelaeologists, there still remain many caves and galleries awaiting discovery on the Spanish side. No one who knows anything about spelaeology will be in the least surprised that a chain of caves cannot be explored from top to bottom in a season or two. Fresh difficulties are encountered at each step, and it is not only courage, initiative and endurance that are needed to overcome them, but more and still more equipment as well. The exploration of Pierre Saint-Martin has been going on for four years, but it took seven years to finish Henne-Morte— 1940-1947—and Cigalère, which Casteret entered for the first time in 1931, has not yet yielded all its secrets.

In 1953, a few miles from where Lévi's teams were working in the La Verna cave, some young French and Belgian spelaeologists were penetrating into the unexplored parts of the Cigalère pot-hole, which had been known to exist since 1938 but which were inaccessible through lack of suitable equipment.

The atmosphere is much the same at all spelaeology centres. At Pierre Saint-Martin the teams meet at the village of Licq-Atheray; the Licq-Atheray of the Cigalère pot-hole is Sentein, where there is a small café in which those who are bitten with cave fever meet over a bottle of Izarra, the famous Basque liqueur with flecks of gold in it. From there you have to walk to reach another small village, a world's end village like Sainte-Engrâce. This is Bentaillou, which is more than six thousand five hundred feet up. The entrance to the Cigalère pot-hole is to be found a little farther on and it looks rather like a stone porch thirty feet high.

Here you have no need of a complicated winch as at Pierre Saint-Martin. All you have to do is walk in, and keep walking as far as you can. But there, of course, the trouble starts. Falls of icy water, some of them as much as sixty feet high, rivers blocking the way which the explorer has to wade through for hours at a stretch with water up to his chest, passages so narrow that you have to squeeze through them like a cat—all the fun of caving is to be found at Cigalère.

Overcome one difficulty, and another appears. Van den Abeele and his team crossed fifteen waterfalls and after hours of being wet, muddy and frozen to the bone they found themselves at the foot of a sixteenth, bigger than all the others, and it defeated them.

The leader of that memorable expedition has described the end of that journey very well:

" Fate willed that we should pay dearly for the joys of

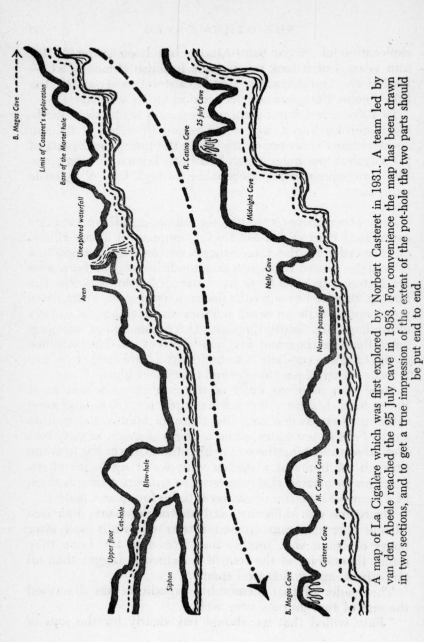

A map of La Cigalère which was first explored by Norbert Casteret in 1931. A team led by van den Abeele reached the 25 July cave in 1953. For convenience the map has been drawn in two sections, and to get a true impression of the extent of the pot-hole the two parts should be put end to end.

B. Magos Cave

Limit of Casteret's exploration

Base of the Martel hole

Unexplored waterfall

Aven

Blow-hole

Cat-hole

Upper floor

Siphon

R. Catino Cave

25 July Cave

Midnight Cave

Nelly Cave

Narrow passage

M. Cosyns Cave

Casteret Cave

B. Magos Cave

discovery. The headroom in the passage soon became less, and though there was a moment when we hoped to see the ceiling rise again it went on dropping inexorably until there was a clearance of only *twelve* inches above the water.

"'Great fun, this!' said my companion, as he crawled into the tunnel.

"We had to make our way along the river bed like snakes, with water seeping down our necks and into our sleeves. It's an absolutely beastly sensation and it lasted for three quarters of an hour, during which we made only about a hundred yards headway. When we got out of it at last, it was only to find ourselves at the foot of a waterfall twelve feet high.

"Here the cave became gigantic once again. A shaft down which the water poured and where the rock surface peeled off in our hands led us to the foot of another drop beyond which we could see two more waterfalls still to come. 'If we get past them we shall be at the fifteenth,' one of us said. To our great astonishment we reached the top of the fourteenth without too much difficulty, after climbing two overhanging spurs ten and fifteen feet high respectively. Then we straightway attacked the fifteenth, which was easy enough to scale, but the rock was crumbling and came away underfoot. We spent more than a quarter of an hour overcoming this obstacle and then used a rope to help the others up. We then pushed ahead and once again we had to crawl through the water over sharp pebbles which cut our hands and tore our clothes. Twenty minutes of crawling on our stomachs, a more disagreeable experience even than the first time, brought us into a cave where the largest waterfall in the whole Cigalère pot-hole was making the most appalling din. 'It must be getting on for sixty feet,' my companion said as he started to climb it.

"The rest of the party had arrived in the meantime, to tell us that they had discovered a vast upper floor and had been able to avoid the series of 'cat-holes' which we had struggled through so unnecessarily.

"Up above us, my companion was baulked some fifty feet

up the waterfall. He tried everything but could not get farther and had to come down again. Then I tried my luck. It was an extremely tricky climb and when I reached the spot where my predecessor had to give up I found myself facing an absolutely smooth stretch of rock. My companion now rejoined me and together we tried to find a means of forcing our way through. There was six feet to go at most and beyond that our difficulties seemed to disappear. ' It's no use trying to get through this way,' my companion said, ' and besides it would be madness. It looks quite hopeless from where I am, and if you fall . . . You may be able to get through the waterfall, but you'll have to be careful because there's no proper hold anywhere.'

" ' I'll take good care,' I told him, but I got nowhere. The force of the water drove me back all the time. ' You'd better give up, old chap,' he said. ' If you lose your hold, you're done for.' So I came back to the only place I had a firm foothold, and we lost no time in getting down. The rest of the team had been kicking their heels down below waiting for us to get through, and they were very disappointed to see us come back. ' Perhaps one of these gentlemen would like to try it for himself,' my companion said ironically. But no one volunteered and we started to make our way back. Before we left the Twenty-Fifth of July cave, as we christened it, we placed a small plaque with this inscription on a cairn which we had built for the purpose:

" ' The Caving Club of France and Belgium. This cave was the farthest point reached by (then follows the names of the members of the expedition) on 25 July 1953.'

" After that we sounded the retreat and started back."

Van Abeele's story was far from finished. There was the journey back to the surface, involving all the difficulties they had met on the outward trip, but now they were tired and their enthusiasm had ebbed, and when they reached the village of Bentaillou they were plastered with mud from head to foot and quite unrecognisable.

Perhaps it may be asked why a spelaeologist of Casteret's achievements went only half the distance in 1933 that these

young men covered twenty years later and why he stopped
at the ninth waterfall leaving it to those who came after him
to find another six. The answer can be found in the simple
matter of equipment. Casteret, for example, at that time did
not possess the poles which are indispensable for climbing
waterfalls. Rope ladders are quite useless and what you
need for the climb is a set of detachable poles which can be
fitted together to make the required length. The rope ladder
is then attached and the poles act as a wall for the ladder
to lean against. The climb is obviously still risky as the poles
often swing dangerously, but it is the best arrangement so
far devised.

I have already mentioned that a good spelaeologist must
be a good swimmer, a good diver and a good climber, all
rolled into one, and for dealing with the Cigalère pot-hole I
think it would be best to add to the list, " and a good acrobat
as well."[1]

IN BELGIUM

Every Belgian tourist knows the caves at Han, Rochefort
and Remouchamps. He can even make a conducted tour of
them, and though they are very different from the caves explored by spelaeologists, they are extremely beautiful all the
same. Belgium also possesses a number of holes which are of
interest to caving enthusiasts, the most important being the
Trou Bernard, discovered in 1949 by a Brussels cameraman,
Bernard Magos. There is also a cave named after him in the
Cigalère pot-hole.

Like most underground explorers I paid a visit to the
Trou Bernard, which is four hundred feet deep. It is certainly dangerous because heavy rains turn it into a sewer

[1] In August 1954 van den Abeele and his companions returned to
the Cigalère pot-hole and reached the twenty-fifth waterfall. Un-
happily, an eighteen-year-old Belgian, Michel de Donnea, was killed
while helping to save some members of the team who had been
trapped by a sudden rise in the river.

and water rushes down. We spent thirteen hours there, but some young people who had gone down in bad weather were only rescued thanks to the help of the fire brigade, and in 1952 a man from Liége was caught unawares by falls of water and broke a leg. It now appears that our parachute commandos are going to make it their training ground in the very near future.

Accidents happen every year, sometimes with tragic consequences, in spite of the precautions taken. But I do not feel that this is any reason for banning spelaeology. I say that advisedly because death will always hover near adventure—were it not so, it would no longer be adventure. Is mountaineering to be banned because falls happen often enough? Or bathing and swimming, because scores of unfortunate people are drowned every year? And what of motoring; shall we stop that because accidents happen? Put like that, it sounds silly enough.

Perhaps we give too much thought at times to our physical safety. Let a man harden his heart or lose his soul; there will be no protest. Perhaps it would be better if there were. Ask me to choose between the man who dies in the darkness of a cave, but with joy in his heart, and the man who takes good care of himself but destroys his moral being, and my choice is already made. And Loubens, I make bold to say, the greatest of all those who have died for spelaeology, offers proof in eternity of a life that is an example to others.

What an inspiration he is! I would never say " Take care " to anyone who told me that Loubens was his ideal. I should be glad to know him, because he would be a true man.

Chapter Eight

1954

THE PADLOCK IS PLACED
ON THE EMPTY TOMB

THE picture is complete and ready for its frame—a portrait of Pierre Saint-Martin and the men who explored it, of happiness and of tragedy.

The first descent, the great discoveries, the justification of spelaeology, scientific and otherwise, Loubens's death, the fierce dramatic struggle to bring his body to the surface, all have their place. So, too, that heartrending moment when José Bidegain collapsed in the mud sobbing with exhaustion. Then he fainted, as much from happiness, I thought, as from the effects of the superhuman effort he had made—happiness at having striven in the noblest of all causes, that of charity.

Mairey rushed to him, while Labeyrie, Lépineux and Delteil stood round anxiously. "Is it serious?" someone asked. "No, it can't be with a man of his stamina." There were things to be done—to ask Lagrave if they might bring Bidegain to his hut, and then to make sure that the coffin was securely fastened to the cable, now that it had reached the top of the shaft.

It was bitterly cold. Rain had followed the snow which had fallen in the night, but there were still large white patches of it on the ground, making the Pierre Saint-Martin ridge look desolate.

We were all exhausted, too tired to talk, our minds a blank; we thought nothing, we felt nothing. If there was

anything to be done, we did it rather like Bidegain working
in the shaft that night, mechanically with only one thought
in mind—" Bring Loubens up . . . Bring Loubens up."
Now that he had been brought up, he was a dead man like
any other, and our only thought was to save Bidegain.

It was half an hour before he recovered consciousness. He
stirred, opened his eyes and moved his lips, like a boxer
recovering from a knockout. He was incoherent at first and
we wondered rather foolishly if his brain had been affected
—that sort of thing had been known to happen. But those
who had been members of the team in 1951 and 1952 remembered that after the accident to Loubens, Tazieff had made
a slow and difficult ascent and when he reached the top he
began to talk disjointedly, staring all round him with hag-
gard eyes. He had been like that for ten minutes.

With Bidegain it lasted about ten minutes, too. Then he
became more like normal, talking more easily and con-
nectedly. A reporter took down one of the first things he
said and sent it to his paper. " This is no time to collapse.
I gave my word . . ."

That was coherent enough, and good to hear; all the more
so as he was still lying stretched out on the stones, his hands
paralysed and his back torn and bruised. Lépineux breathed
again; Bidegain was not for the mortuary, he would not even
have to go to hospital.

It was now one thirty, and Lépineux, Lévi and
Quéffelec made for the shaft entrance where the container
was still jammed. Lévi worked it loose, and then there
was only one more thing to be done. With Quéffelec and his
friends down in the *doline* and some men from Licq-Atheray
stationed up top, they slowly hoisted the metal container
with the help of ropes out of the shaft and up to the top of
the *doline*. When the container lay on level ground at last,
I felt our hearts all beating a little more quickly, and putting
on my surplice I said a *De Profundis* and asked everyone to
join me in three *Aves*.

I do not know how a moment of perfection comes to be.
Can we ever know that it will come before it has come? So

reaches the surface
oubens's fall. *Above*:
ey gives instructions
e men below, before
g down the shaft him-
Below: Mairey and
Cosyns.

After bringing Loubens's coffin to the surface, José Bidegain is taken
to Lagrave's hut by Mairey and Loriaux.

many things outside ourselves, so many influences play their parts with extreme simplicity, and it only needs a little thing to dispel it all. Yet suddenly I felt that such a moment was upon us. Round the poor little coffin, dented and scratched, muddy, dirty, we were as one fervently praying to God Almighty for our dead friend, our minds free from dissension, envy, meanness, and united in a new spirit, because we had striven together to bring our friend to the surface, because each had played his part without waste of words, above all because as the prayers passed our lips the sun broke through the clouds at last, and because José Bidegain straightened up, tried to rise to his feet, succeeded, and came and prayed with us.

GOING DOWN INTO THE VALLEY

It was just before three that Sauveur Bouchet, our kindly host from the hotel at Licq-Atheray, arrived with several others to take the container down to Sainte-Engrâce, where the Romanesque church had been prepared. The way down was difficult; the track was muddy and full of ruts, and it took an hour and all their skill to reach the village without accident.

The body was taken from the container and placed in a wooden coffin, which was then put inside another coffin made of zinc, and Loubens who for two years had lain apart now took his place among the other dead, according to tradition and the wishes of his mother and father.

I had written to his father, and he had come at once, alone as Loubens's mother was unable to make the tiring journey. The scene in the church was painful. Loubens's father broke down beside his son's coffin and, unable to master his grief, he said something which astonished us all: " How you have made us suffer, Marcel, these last two years."

He explained a little later to those around him. " I'm so happy to see Marcel on the way to Mazères-du-Salat. That is his home and there will be nothing more to disturb him. I am deeply grateful to all those who have kept their promise to carry out our wishes and have performed this tremendous task. The thought of Pierre Saint-Martin will no longer torment us, now that it has ceased to hold our boy prisoner."

Loubens remained throughout the Monday in the church of Licq-Atheray, where he had stayed before his tragic accident and where he had left his friends for a moment, remarking, " I'm just going to say a prayer to Our Lord of Sainte-Engrâce."

The next day, Tuesday, undertakers came from Pau to remove him to Mazères-du-Salat, where he was laid to rest among his own people in the cemetery beside the church, and at last his mother could pray beside his grave.

PACKING UP

Up at Pierre Saint-Martin there were still things to do. It was three in the afternoon. I had said Mass near Lagrave's hut, where Bidegain was resting. Some of the party had already gone down to the valley, but those who had played the leading parts in the events we had just lived through were still about, and there were still two men at the bottom of the shaft waiting to be brought up.

This was no easy task because the cable refused to go down unweighted and kept catching on overhanging rocks and jamming at every turn.

" Heavens above," cried Quéffelec in exasperation, " what's the matter with it now?" But there was nothing for it—there had to be a weight on the end of the cable and that meant sending a man down, hardly a pleasant prospect as none of us had had any sleep the night before. But in the end a young Belgian called Loriaux, who had never been down before, volunteered, which was a piece of luck for us and an experience for him. He got down safely, and then late in the evening the men at the bottom were able to come up.

THE PADLOCK ON THE EMPTY TOMB   145

Brosset, who was a close friend of Loubens and who had gone down to pay his respects for the last time, was the first to reach the surface and in good shape. "Any news?" he asked at once. A letter was waiting for him from his wife, telling him that while he had been camping at the bottom of the shaft she had presented him with a son. "Hurray!" he cried. "Casteret shall be godfather." It was his second child and Brosset seemed to have a taste for spelaeologists as god-fathers, because Marcel Loubens had acted in this capacity to his first child.

*   *   *   *   *

There is a little door at the entrance to the Pierre Saint-Martin hole, a door that is fastened by a padlock. Lévi went down the *doline* for the last time. The winch had been taken away and the cable wound up and in a few short hours the place had assumed its winter look. Lévi was pale, with a three day growth of beard. "Hurry up," someone shouted. "Let's get it over." Lévi closed the shutter carefully, put the padlock on and turned the key on an empty tomb, on a cave where the elements could do their worst until next summer, now that there was no one down there.

Would they ever return to Pierre Saint-Martin? The Spaniards were not very keen on it, especially as some of the caves still waiting to be explored lie on their side of the border. But there were Casteret and the others to be reckoned with. At first they seemed to think that it was all over and that they would never go back; after all, there were other caves to be explored. But as the months went by they were not so sure. Their thoughts kept going back to Pierre Saint-Martin. They felt that they could not leave unexplored whatever lay beyond the Navarre cave, and that they would have to go down there once again.

Pierre Saint-Martin was now deserted. Lévi had gone, Bidegain, too, and Ballandreaux, who had been the last to come up. There was no one except the shepherds, the sheep, the dogs, the crows and the frontier stones, silent witnesses of bygone quarrels. Then, in due course, men and beasts went down to the valley and the shelter of the villages. A great silence hung over the mountains, a silence like that of the cemetery at Mazères-du-Salat, where gravediggers were preparing to lower Marcel Loubens, among his own people at last, into a grave which must have seemed so tiny to him. "We invaded that silence," said Casteret, deeply moved, "we invaded it for a brief moment, for we had sworn to take you from the depths of that vast inhuman cave and bring you back to your native village."

Silence. Is there a better word with which to close a book dedicated to the least talkative of men?

APPENDICES

A Short Spelaeological Dictionary

Nominal List of the Teams at Pierre Saint-Martin

A Spelaeologist's Equipment

The Pierre Saint-Martin Camp

Science goes down the Pot-hole

Official Assistance to Spelaeology

Pierre Saint-Martin, 1955

A SHORT SPELAEOLOGICAL DICTIONARY

AUTO-LIFT Small device which allows the spelaeologist to attach himself to the cable and climb up and down it by the strength of his wrists. It is fitted with a brake. In 1954 Bidegain used an auto-lift designed by Quéffelec to free the container and then to bring it up from point 520 to the surface.

AVEN Local word used in the neighbourhood of Causses (S.W. of the Cevennes between the departments of Dordogne and Lot) to denote a pot-hole.

BLOW-HOLE Hole where wind blows up from below, generally with some force, or narrow opening along which a current of air passes; may be caused by air suction. At Pierre Saint-Martin there is a cave which has been given this name (Trou Souffleur). It was explored by the Lyons scouts and Father Attout.

CABLE CAP Cap designed to prevent the end of the cable from being caught up in cracks or fissures. A cylinder is attached to protect the microphone and earphones when the cable is being used unweighted.

CAIRN Small mound of stones built by explorers (subterranean or otherwise) to mark their route. Serves as a sign-post. A word of Irish origin, denoting a tumulus of earth or stones, built by the Celts.

CALCITE Natural carbonate of calcium.

CAT-HOLE (*chatière* or *étroiture*) Passage with or without a way through, along which there is only room to crawl. A great many in Pierre Saint-Martin; they are found in the rock walls separating one cave from another.

CAVE PEARL Small ball of limestone varying in size from a pea to a hen's egg. Also called a pisolite. Some pure calcium carbonate pisolites are astonishingly white.

CAYOLLARD Shepherd's hut, without windows, made of stones placed loosely on top of one another, in the Basque and Béarn countries.

CHIMNEY Vertical passage in a cave. Can vary in size. The shaft of Pierre Saint-Martin is a chimney of 1,115 feet. The walls of the chimney are not necessarily smooth. Numerous ledges or platforms can help or hinder passage. Some chimneys are spiral in form.

CHIMNEY SWEEPING A means of descent, in which the back is pressed against one side of the shaft, and the feet against the other. It results in all loose stones being swept up.

CHORUM Synonym for pot-hole in some regions.

CLAMP Used to fasten the thimble (which is itself strengthened by a metal eye inside it) at the end of the cable. The spelaeologist is attached to this thimble by two hooks. Loubens had only one clamp. Two are now used.

CLAUSTROPHOBIA There is cave sickness, as well as sea and mountain sickness. Cave sickness involves complete loss of appetite, and any food taken is brought up immediately.

CORNICE (or ledge) Rocky projection in a cave or chimney, which affords a foothold. Varies in size and angle of slope. In Pierre Saint-Martin there are two large ledges, one at 260 and the other at 700 feet.

DIACLASE Fracture enlarged by the action of water, and resembling a vertical fault, usually narrow but often of considerable height.

DIHEDRON V-shaped formation (with the V upright or inverted) between two layers of rock. The container which brought Loubens's body to the surface was trapped for a long time in a dihedron at point 520.

DOLINE Circular depression in rocky ground, often in the form of a very large funnel, at the bottom of which a shaft is sometimes found. Pierre Saint-Martin has a *doline* thirty feet deep, forming an unmistakable gap in the Franco-Spanish frontier. The entrance to the hole itself is three feet from the bottom on the Spanish side and is minute.

FAULT Break in the continuity of rock strata, caused by a vertical fracture.

FISTULEUSE A stalagtite no thicker than a pencil and having the same diameter for its whole length.

FLUORESCEIN Strong chemical colouring matter. Shortly before his death, Loubens put about a hundred pounds of fluorescein into the river at the bottom of the hole, and in the following year (1953) Casteret put forty-five pounds. Thanks to the colouring of the water it has been possible to discover where the underground river flows out into the Sainte-Engrâce valley. It took eighteen days in 1952, and twenty-one days in 1953, for the coloured water to reach the surface.

GAVE Word of Béarnese origin meaning mountain stream or torrent. The Sainte-Engrâce or Oloron *gave* flows near Pierre Saint-Martin. In the Pyrenees the best-known *gave* is that of Pau.

GIANT'S CAULDRON Large round hollow, formed in calcareous rock by a whirlpool of water or by the abrasive action of stones caught up in it.

GLACIER Can occur underground. Casteret has explored the world's highest underground glaciers.

GOURS Natural basin, the sides of which have been covered by the progressive accumulation of calcareous deposit. Name given in Auvergne to lakes formed in old volcanic craters.

HYDROGEOLOGICAL PASSAGE The Pierre Saint-Martin hole is one.

LAKE Stretch of underground water which has sometimes to be crossed by swimming or in a rubber canoe.

LAMINOIR A wide but very low fault, which makes crawling essential.

LAPIAZ Carving on the surface of the rock caused by erosion and the chemical dissolution of calcareous rock. Less scientifically, very much like a rocky sponge, which flowers and sometimes spreads for several square miles. Like the lapiaz in the Pic d'Anie grotto. Also called lapies.

LIMESTONE Rock rich in carbonate of lime. Chalk and marble are calcareous (limestone) rocks. Water containing carbonate of calcium, when passing through limestone, releases on contact with air a carbonic gas, causing a crystalline deposit—stalactite or stalagmite.

MARL Mixture of calcareous soil and clay. Calcareous marls contain at least fifty per cent. of limestone, clay marls from sixty to seventy-five per cent. of clay. There are also silicic and magnesium marls.

NEVE Solid snow which forms in the course of a season and often closes the bottom of a hole. Near Pierre Saint-Martin numerous holes ended in *névés* (the Trou du Vent, for example).

OUISTITI Name given by reporters at Pierre Saint-Martin to the auto-lift invented by Quéffelec, because whoever used it had to adopt a posture like that of the animal of that name. (A marmoset found in Brazil, which hangs by its tail.)

OUTFALL The mouth of a subterranean river. N.B. It never applies to the source. The subterranean river of the Pierre Saint-Martin hole came to the surface in the Kakouetta valley, near the village of Sainte-Engrâce, in France, at a place called Bentia.

PARPAING Large stone which becomes detached from the rock wall and constitutes a real danger. Ertaud, the cameraman, narrowly escaped being killed by a *parpaing* while filming in the Pierre Saint-Martin hole.

PLATFORM Synonym for cornice or ledge, but larger.

POT-HOLE Every deep hole. The Pierre Saint-Martin hole is the deepest in the world, but not the most extensive. Its galleries, on the French side, are over three thousand yards long and reach to a depth of about 2,400 feet. Near Grenoble there is a pot-hole known as the Dent de Crolles, which has some ten miles of galleries and a depth of about 2,100 feet.

PROFILE Apparatus invented by Lépineux and designed to bring the container through the difficult parts of the shaft undamaged. Also called a pulley-arm.

RAILLIERE Heap of fallen stones, pile of rubble.

REDAN Rock forming a salient.

RIMAIX or *RIMAYLLE* Crevasse between ice and rock. Dangerous in time of thaw.

RUBBLE CONE Accumulation of stones of all sizes, caused by subterranean falls of rock. It is more or less stable and is often to be found under the opening of the shaft itself. May be up to three hundred feet in height. Marcel Loubens was killed by falling on the rubble cone at the bottom of the Lépineux hole. After a fall of thirty feet he rolled from stone to stone for a further hundred feet. This fatal fall was only checked by the intervention of Labeyrie.

SCHIST   Rock with foliated structure. Schist is one of the oldest deposits. At Pierre Saint-Martin it was found under the caves and galleries with limestone above it.

SHAFT   Synonym for hole, chimney, *aven*, and *chorum*. Always contains fractures, cracks and often faults.

SIPHON   Place where the water reaches the roof, thus forcing the underground explorer to dive right under the water. Some *siphons* are sixty yards long. The Lyons scouts, who are expert at rope-ladder descents, are also specialists at crossing *siphons*. Extremely dangerous.

SOUM   The word used in the Pyrenees, Basque and Béarn countries for mountain top or summit. Near to Pierre Saint-Martin is the Soum de Lèche or Milky Summit, so called because hundreds of sheep graze on it.

STALACTITE   Calcareous deposit suspended from the roof of a cave. See definition of limestone.

STALACTITE (ECCENTRIC)   Calcium carbonate deposit (therefore white), the tree-like formation of which defies all the laws of gravity and whose construction still remains unexplained. Only one cave in the Pierre Saint-Martin hole contains tree-like stalactites; it is a small cave opening out of the Navarre cave, the Spanish branch of the hole.

STALAGMITE   Calcareous deposit rising from the floor of a cave. Formed by the slow and continuous fall of water. Columns are formed when stalagmite and stalactite join.

STRATUM   A layer formed by deposits.

SWALLOW   Place where water disappears into the rock.

WINCH   A humorous definition might be: "an apparatus for winding a cable, indispensable for the exploration of vertical shafts, while always giving the greatest possible trouble to the spelaeologists who use it." This would be less than the truth in the case of Pierre Saint-Martin.

NOMINAL LIST OF THE TEAMS
AT PIERRE SAINT-MARTIN

1950   Cosyns (leader), Lépineux, Labeyrie, Lévi, Loubens, Occhialini, Théodor. *A French, Italian and Belgian team.*

1951   Cosyns (leader), Ertaud (cameraman), Janssens (engineer), Labeyrie, Laisse (the youngest), Lépineux, Lévi (steward), Loubens, Occhialini, Pérot, Petitjean, Tazieff (cameraman). *A French, Italian and Belgian team.*

1952   Cosyns (leader), Janssens, Labeyrie, Laisse, Lévi, Loubens, Louis (mechanic), Mairey (doctor), Morizot, Occhialini, Théodor, Treuthard, Tazieff (cameraman). *A French, Italian and Belgian team.*

1953   Accocce, Attout (priest), Ballandreaux—Milou and Georges —(Lyons scouts), Bidegain, Brosset (great friend of Marcel Loubens), Casteret (leader below ground), Delteil, Epelly (Lyons scout), Ertaud, Janssens, Laisse, Lépineux, Letrône (Lyons scout), Lévi, Louis, Mairey, Morizot, Naudin (Quéffelec's assistant on the winch), Occhialini, Quéffelec (engineer), Rossini, Théodor, Treuthard, Vergnes, Professor Llopis, Assens, Eloséguy, Ondarra, Termes. *A French, Italian, Belgian and Spanish team.*

1954   Accocce, Attout, Ballandreaux—Milou—(leader of Lyons scouts), Bidegain, Brosset, Casteret, Choupin, Delteil, Isola (Quéffelec's mechanic), Mauer, Laisse, Lépineux, Letrône, Lévi (leader of expedition), Loriaux, Louis, Mairey, Perillaus (cook), Quéffelec, Rossini, Vergnes (cameraman). *A French and Belgian team.*

A SPELAEOLOGIST'S EQUIPMENT

A spelaeologist's equipment, whoever he may be and whether he is exploring a large or a small hole, will always be determined by the conditions prevailing at the bottom; damp, cold, *siphons,* mud, etc. First essential for everybody is an impressive array of vests and pullovers. Next, a one-piece boiler suit, with no bits and pieces to get caught up, and often a waterproof overall as well, which is very useful for crossing waterfalls. If there are *siphons* to be dealt with, a complete frogman's outfit is essential —diving suit, underwater goggles, rubber fins for the feet, oxygen bottle on the back and watertight torch.

A helmet to protect the head—some members of the Pierre Saint-Martin expedition used a jet pilot's helmet, which is the strongest, and being made of spun glass is more solid than steel.

A lamp or lamps are also indispensable. First a headlamp fixed to the helmet; second, a torch carried in the hand or hung from the chest. Some spelaeologists like electric torches, others (the Lyons scouts, for example) prefer acetylene lamps.

In addition to personal gear there is equipment belonging to the expedition; rope ladders, cable, mountaineering gear, rubber canoe, and telephone or walkie-talkie—and at Pierre Saint-Martin, of course, the steel cable and electric-driven winch.

The spelaeologist, and particularly the spelaeologist who has not had much experience, must never forget that something may always go wrong with some part of his equipment. He should remember to take along a cigarette lighter, and some matches in a waterproof box, for electric batteries often behave in the strangest ways; also plenty of rope, and some medical supplies.

Obviously an expedition of the size of that to Pierre Saint-Martin must have cost a great deal of money—more than a million French francs, and that was for one year's expedition alone. These heavy expenses have been covered in part by publishing accounts of the expedition in the newspapers, by the sale of photographs and the hiring of films; gross receipts from these sources have totalled 600,000 French francs in all.

We must never forget that material equipment is one thing, and moral equipment another. No one goes pot-holing without some training. A good spelaeologist must not only have endurance and be able to bear cold, hunger and damp; he must also be prepared to do a little swimming and a little Alpine climbing, and to maintain the suppleness and agility which only regular training can bestow. He must have plenty of patience, and a liking for being alone in complete darkness. For a spelaeologist has often to stay for hours by himself in the depths of the cave waiting for someone to join him. If it gets too much for him and he loses his head, he may well cause a needless accident. What is more serious is that losing his head when he finds that he is lost spells certain disaster. A sense of direction and, above all, a sense of discipline are both equally essential below ground.

The spelaeologist will not think only of himself. There are others waiting to follow where he is going. For their benefit, and for the good of the team as a whole, he will mark out his route and signpost the dangerous places. A lone wolf or a dreamer will always make a bad underground explorer. What it amounts to is that anyone who thinks that only physical training is necessary for spelaeological work will get nowhere. He will only be half a spelaeologist and a constant danger to others.

Spelaeology is no picnic; it calls for great effort on the part of its enthusiasts and it is only once that effort has been made that the explorer will know the joy of complete victory over nature and over self, and joy is something more and something quite different from mere pleasure.

THE PIERRE SAINT-MARTIN CAMP

At Pierre Saint-Martin the camp was not, as might be thought, just a few tents pitched round the *doline* and nothing more. The main camp, in fact, was situated some hundred yards away from the pot-hole at an altitude of six thousand feet, and only the winch lay at the edge of the *doline*. The generator was on a small platform between the winch and the camp. The mess tent, the " Panmunjom tent" of 1953, stood next to Lagrave's hut near frontier stone 262. The telephone line ran for half a mile before reaching the hut belonging to the Tham-Tham brothers, where the gendarmes had their headquarters. It was from this same hut that radio contact was maintained with the people in the valley at Sainte-Engrâce. There was also a Spanish camp, close to the *doline* but on Spanish soil.

SCIENCE GOES DOWN THE POT-HOLE

Spelaeology is a sport and a dangerous sport, like mountaineering. But it is more than that; it has also a scientific role to play.

PREHISTORY Thanks to the exploration of caves and grottoes we know more today about the lives of the world's first inhabitants. We know of their interest in art, for the drawings and figures which have been found in caves show keen powers of observation and the ability for self-expression.

UNDERGROUND METEOROLOGY The temperature of underground caves is not the same as that recorded above ground. The laws governing the world underground offer an interesting field of study to the research worker, and phenomena connected with ionisation and telluric radiation, which are matters of common interest today as certain fields of cancer research are allied to them, can be better observed in caves.

HYDROGEOLOGY Studies of underground erosion form the basis of such projects as irrigation, the harnessing of underground water and its utilisation in hydro-electric power schemes. In 1935, while exploring the Martel hole where there is a waterfall, Casteret gave permission for it to be diverted into the open air and sent through a conduit which goes down the mountain side and links up with the central hydro-electric system at Eylie.

ZOOLOGY Insects—*carnicoli*—have been found at the bottom of caves. Entomologists have not been able to find insects of the same species living above ground, for they disappeared from there millions of years ago. Bats, too, can best be studied in caves.

OFFICIAL ASSISTANCE TO
SPELAEOLOGY

Spelaeology, like archaeology and geography, is a science which calls for both the specialist and the enthusiast, and in face of its steady growth in importance some governments have been willing to subsidise major expeditions.

The French Army arrived at the Henne-Morte pot-hole, which was being explored by a team of twenty-five spelaeologists, with trucks and jeeps detailed for the transport of specialist equipment. In addition, there were a hundred infantrymen helping the team for the duration of the expedition.

At Pierre Saint-Martin the Air Force, with their base at Pau, gave valuable help by dropping forty-eight parachutes. A unit of airborne troops supplied parachute harnesses and special helmets, while the gendarmerie provided a radio link with the rest of the country, and the Public Works Department, the Post Office and the French Electricity Board all helped in the common task.

PIERRE SAINT-MARTIN, 1955

The final cave to be discovered at the bottom of the Pierre Saint-Martin hole, the La Verna cave, lies just below the steep, tree-covered Arpidia gorge, half-way between Sainte-Engrâce and the entrance to the pot-hole. Since last June the French Electricity Board's engineers have done important work there, their aim being to penetrate from the gorge into the La Verna cave, which spelaeologists discovered 2,388 feet down in the bowels of the earth. If they can harness the Pierre Saint-Martin underground river they will have at their command a waterfall nearly two thousand feet high, which would supply a major hydro-electric installation to be built in the Sainte-Engrâce valley. Industry could be brought to the Oloron valley or the French Railways supplied with electric power.

Tests showed that the rock is about two hundred and sixty feet thick, and last June work began on cutting a way through and building an enormous tunnel. This should already have reached a length of two hundred and sixty feet by mid-August, and it is estimated that when it joins the La Verna cave it will be nearly four hundred feet long. The work should be completed by the end of the year, before the worst of the winter begins. The engineers will then be able to measure the power of the underground river before reporting on the advisability of building a hydro-electric plant.

Members of the Pierre Saint-Martin expedition are already planning for 1956 a new series of explorations starting from the artificial tunnel, which will make things very much easier. It will no longer be necessary to use the dangerous Pierre Saint-Martin shaft, and it will be easier to penetrate the network of caves which stretch for more than six miles along the subterranean river.

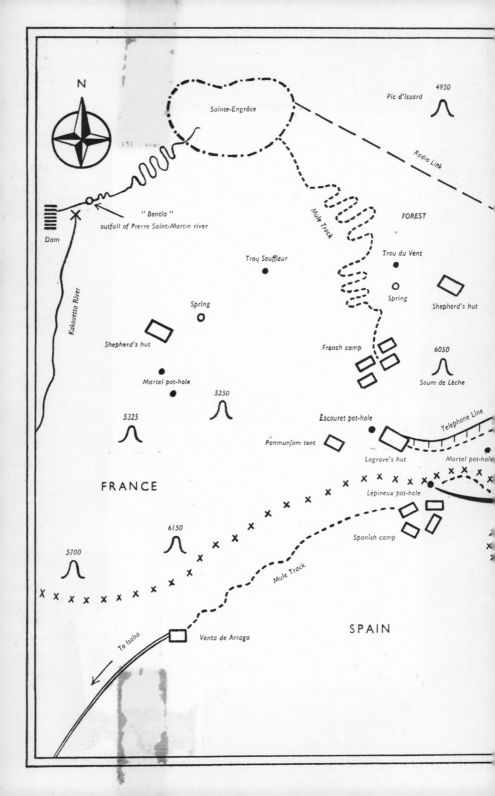